MINISTRY IN DAILY LIFE

a practical guide for congregations

◆

WILLIAM E. DIEHL

an alban institute publication

The Publications Program of The Alban Institute is assisted by a grant from Trinity Church, New York City.

Library of Congress Catalog Card #96-85342
ISBN 1-56699-172-2

CONTENTS

This book is for and about the people who will have the most influential role to play in the twenty-first century—the Christian laity and the clergy who will be supporting them.

How times have changed since the church-growth heyday of the 1950s! As Americans emerged from World War II to start new families in burgeoning residential developments, their cultural habit of church going caused membership rolls to swell. New congregations started, and existing ones knocked down walls to add space. The laity helped by serving on committees, teaching Sunday school, being advisors for the youth group, singing in the choir, and ushering. Largely, they were passive pew sitters when it came to relating their faith to their daily lives. Someone refers to them as "pew potatoes."

Times Have Changed

Who could have dreamed then that in less than forty years, the membership in the mainline denominations would have dropped precipitously? Who could have predicted that church growth would come primarily from independent, storefront congregations, some of which are now megachurches? Who could have foreseen the heavy political influence of well-organized religious conservatives in all levels of government? Who could have dreamed of the heavy influx into all parts of America of non-Christian immigrants who rightly insist upon equal religious freedoms under our Constitution? Who would have dared to predict that the admonitions of the pope would frequently be ignored by large numbers of Roman Catholic laity and some clergy? Who could have foreseen the assault upon traditional Christian values by many elements of our society? Or the breakdown of our traditional understanding of family?

The list could go on and on. What is most unfortunate, however, is that in this vast sea of change, the mainline churches have consistently struggled to find ways to restore things to the way they were in the 1950s. Change has been seen as a problem to be resisted, not as an opportunity for a new form of mission and ministry.

By now, however, it is obvious to all but the most strident denominational traditionalist that the Christian church must change its approach to ministry. It's a different world out there, and the national denominational offices simply do not have enough financial resources nor enough clergy to do ministry in this different world while an increasingly aging laity continue to sit passively in the pews and sing the old hymns.

The Greatest Transformation

In his best-selling book, *The Once and Future Church: Reinventing the Congregation for a New Mission Frontier*, Loren Mead writes, "We are at the front edges of the greatest transformation of the church that has occurred in 1,600 years. It is by far the greatest change that the church has ever experienced in America; it may eventually make the transformation of the Reformation look like a ripple in a pond."[1]

The leading edge of this "greatest transformation of the church" has been developing over the past forty years. It was originally called "lay ministry" and, in most instances, referred to the laity taking a more active role in their congregations, both in service and decision making. The term "ministry of the laity" followed, which suggested that lay persons had a ministry beyond the walls of their congregations. More recently, in an effort to affirm the clergy-laity partnership, the term has become "Ministry in Daily Life," which is the language of this book.

The lay renewal movement began primarily because those Christians who were trying to take the Gospel seriously were increasingly concerned that their Sunday experiences in church did not seem to connect with their weekday experiences in the world. As the movement to connect faith and daily life grew, it was seen largely as another program of the church. In some cases, it was seen as distracting from the "real work of the church," which was maintaining the traditional patterns of church life.

It is my conviction that the Holy Spirit has been leading the church toward a new style of mission and ministry in these past forty years and we haven't realized it. It is my conviction that the great "transformation of the church" of which Mead writes lies in the role of the laity. In a multicultural, individualistic society that is increasingly indifferent and sometimes hostile to Christianity, it will have to be the laity who in their daily lives carry forward Christ's admonition to "go into all the world." The mission field is right outside the doors of our congregations, and it is the laity who will have to be the missionaries. There is no other way open to the church.

If the laity are to be the missionaries, dramatic changes have to happen in the traditional local church or parish. On the one hand, people who have been very comfortable as pew sitters and who never fret about ministry in their daily lives will not be excited about their new role. It will take time and patience to bring them along. On the other hand, many persons who have suffered through what they consider boring worship services and who have longed for something more vital will find the new role of the laity exciting. Moreover, those congregations that are intentional about Ministry in Daily Life will attract new members. We see it happening already.

The reaction of clergy will also vary. Those who see themselves as leaders in a tightly controlled congregation may well see the transformation as a threat to their ministry. They see ministry as a zero-sum game. They conclude that if all members are in ministry, then the pastor's ministry is diminished. Other pastors will see Ministry in Daily Life as multiplying their ministry. They will see their role more clearly defined than before. They will see themselves as the ones who provide the spiritual nourishment, the affirmation, and the support for lay members to enter the mission field daily.

New Models for Churches

Bill Easum, in his book *Sacred Cows Make Gourmet Burgers: Ministry Anytime, Anywhere by Anyone*, sees the local church changing from being a tightly controlled organization to one focused on "permission giving." One of the characteristics of permission given by local churches is that they "encourage ministry to be developed at any time, any place, by any one, no matter what."[2] This is the essence of Ministry in Daily Life.

Does this mean that there must be a new organizational structure in the local church? It is too early to tell. In her pioneering book, *The Empowering Church*, Pastor Davida Foy Crabtree describes how her congregation, Colchester Federated Church in Colchester, Connecticut, restructured in order to support the ministries of all its people in the world.[3] It is a remarkable story, but Pastor Crabtree is the first to say that it may not be the model for all congregations.

This book describes how my congregation, the Lutheran Church of the Holy Spirit in Emmaus, Pennsylvania—with virtually no changes in organizational structure—is working to affirm, equip, and support its members for Ministry in Daily Life.

The stories of Colchester Federated Church and Holy Spirit Church are incomplete. They are more like status reports. Both congregations frankly say that they are "on the way" to a new style of congregational mission and ministry that is still not fully developed.

Whether churches change by radical restructuring or gradual evolution, however, the end point is clear. No longer will "the ministry of the laity" be seen as peripheral to the "real work" of the church. It will *be* the real work of the church.

CHAPTER 1

Boundaries All around Us

And now, Lord, look at their threats, and grant to your servants to speak your word with all boldness. (Acts 4:29)

"It Was Not Always This Way"

"Discuss religion in my workplace? Never! It would be like tossing a match into gasoline." So said a successful, middle-aged Episcopal businessman in a seminar I was leading at his church. He was a loyal and active member of his congregation. He gave generously of his time and money to the church. But when he moved from the environment of his church to the environment of his job, he crossed a boundary line. What was acceptable conversation in the church was unacceptable in his job.

It was not always this way. At the turn of the century, businessmen were comfortable being public about their Christian beliefs.

Lynn, a school teacher in my congregation, also crosses a boundary line each week. She teaches fifth graders in our Sunday school and does it well. However, in her public school classroom, any mention of the Christian faith or Christian values is against school district policy. She grieves over this as she encounters children from homes where there appears to be no teaching of values or where the values that are imparted are contrary to Lynn's own. But she must remain silent.

It was not always this way. I recall going through the public school system, from first grade to high school, where every morning one of us took a turn reading to the class from the Bible—usually the book of Psalms. The class then rose to pray the Lord's Prayer and to pledge allegiance to the flag.

Dave, another member of our congregation, gets upset that the large-as-life nativity scene that used to have a place each Christmas in the public square of our little town is no longer permitted. He doesn't like the boundary line that his government has drawn between a Christmas display on a church lawn and that same display in front of the public library. "We used to have nativity scenes all over town," he complains. "Why can't the ACLU leave us alone? Let us enjoy Christmas as we used to!"

In his June 1995 *Quarterly Yoke Letter*, James Newby tells of attending a luncheon at which he sat between the chairman of the Department of Sociology at a major California university and a professor in the School of Social Work at a major eastern university. During luncheon conversation, Newby turned to the professor of the large California university and mentioned that he had just read an interesting article about the tremendous decrease in homicides in Los Angeles County during the 1988 Olympics. He said that the author of the article claimed that prayer had played a vital role in this reduction.

Newby went on to explain that there had been small prayer groups meeting around the city, praying for a peaceful Olympics, and that he felt their prayer seemed to have helped. The professor smiled, began laughing, and "before long the whole table erupted at what seemed to be the most laughable statement any of them had heard in a long time," Newby writes. Newby did not say how it felt to be laughed at by a table of prominent sociologists and educators. Instead, he went on in the newsletter to affirm his conviction in the power of prayer. But, unknowingly, he had crossed a boundary established and shared by at least a segment of the academic community.

It was not always this way. While religion has traditionally been suspect among many intellectuals, seldom was it openly derided in public by a group of highly respected academicians.

While house sitting when our daughter and son-in-law took a short trip to Europe, I became the chauffeur who got our twelve-year-old grandson to Little League games and practices. I was surprised to discover that one of his all-star team practices was scheduled for 10:00 A.M. Sunday. When discussing this with his coach, I was told that with a limited number of playing fields available for a large number of teams, every day had to be scheduled from early morning to dusk. "Unfortunately, sometimes we have to play on Sunday morning," he apologized.

It was not always this way. Time was when no organized sporting events were held on a Sunday. Nor were shopping malls or theaters open. It was the Lord's Day.

What's going on? Why are Christians in America encountering religious boundaries that didn't exist before? The answer, of course, is that this nation is becoming increasingly pluralistic. Just read the names of students graduating from your local high school. There will be young people whose families come from Japan, China, Korea, Southeast Asia, India, Africa, the Middle East, Central and South America. Some families are Christian by virtue of the many years of world missionary work done by the churches of Europe and America. But not all. Some come with other religious beliefs and practices.

Thanks to the First Amendment of the United States Constitution, all are granted the freedom to practice the faith of their choice without any intrusion by their government. For Lynn to share her Christian values in the public school classroom would be an intrusion in the eyes of Jewish and Muslim students and their parents. Nor can the government appear to favor any one particular faith. While my friend Dave bristles at the boundaries set up for the public expression of Christianity, I'm sure he would be outraged if Muslims or Hindus or others were permitted to have their religious displays in front of the public library on their holy days.

But what about the Episcopal businessman? There are no government- or group-imposed boundary lines that keep him from talking about his faith on the job. Who has drawn these boundary lines? There are several factors operating here.

Sources of Boundaries

First, because religion is a very private thing for many, it has been good policy in business settings not to bring up a topic that might be a source of tension. "In business never discuss religion, sex, or politics" has been a maxim for a long time. In other professions, discussion of sex or politics is not as much of a taboo, but religious talk is. James Newby learned that at the luncheon he attended with the academic community. The taboo is strongest in the mainline denominations. Christian evangelicals are much more comfortable than mainline Christians with expressing their faith convictions—even in business.

In his book *U.S. Lifestyles and Mainline Churches*, Tex Sample points out that those who constitute the "Middle" culture in our society, the business and professional people, are generally private in their faith.[4] They function in highly competitive environments and, therefore, tend to be individualistic. Privatism is a companion of individualism.

A second reason for self-imposed boundaries is that we are increasingly recognizing our growing pluralism in America and becoming more sensitive to the feelings of those whose faith differs from ours. As a child in that public school classroom, I did not know that Jewish children do not pray the Lord's Prayer or celebrate Christmas. Our grandchildren know, and they act accordingly. One wonders, however, if Newby had been a Muslim expressing his conviction in prayer, would the academics have laughed at him? Do we live in a society that tends to be more sensitive to the feelings of minority religious groups than of Christians? Are groups more likely to impose boundaries on Christians than on others?

As the traditional boundaries between church and world change, our pluralistic society moves in to challenge and change the respect once accorded the nation's dominant religion. Secular society asks why shopping malls should not be open on Sundays. After all, Christians would not consider closing them from Friday sunset to Saturday sunset out of respect to the Jewish population! And why not let Little League teams play, too?

But in addition to government-imposed, group-imposed, and self-imposed boundaries, there is a third source of boundaries imposed on church members. It is, surprisingly, the church itself. Without going into a detailed analysis of how it all came to be, the fact is that most congregations are inward looking and focused on self-preservation. Highly trained professional leaders are called to minister *to* (not *with*) the members of the congregation who willingly play a passive role. Those few members who do assume active roles in the church are affirmed for their service *to* the congregation. Evangelism has come to mean getting new members *for* the congregation, not taking the Gospel into the world. Stewardship has come to mean giving time and money *to* the congregation, not the responsible use of all our time and all our resources in daily life. The pastor has become the only person who may visit the sick. Social ministry is done by other church professionals. National denominational offices send out missionaries, support seminaries, set professional standards, design educational materials, and, occasionally, speak out on social issues. It has been commonly recognized that the highest call for any Christian is the call into "full-time Christian service," that is, the ordained ministry.

One result of all this is that many local churches have unwittingly drawn a tight boundary line around themselves. Things sacred occur within the boundary. Things secular occur outside the boundary, where evil abounds. Not only are the roles of Christian business persons in the world not affirmed, but at times they are used in sermon illustrations as the embodiment of selfish greed and evil in the "secular" world.

The problem with all of this is that it is unbiblical and certainly not consistent with the model established by Jesus. The gospels are clear about it: Jesus regularly attended the synagogue, but his ministry was in and to the world. He shocked the religious leaders of the day by eating with tax collectors, ministering to prostitutes, and reaching out to the despised Samaritans. He healed the sick, fed the hungry, and spoke about the kingdom of God. His parables were rich with examples of every day living *outside* the synagogue and even involved economic issues. For Jesus, there were no boundaries that limit sharing the faith.

His final command to his followers is recorded three times: "Go and make disciples of all nations" (Matthew 28:19a NIV); "Go into all the world and preach the good news to all creation" (Mark 16:15 NIV); and "You will be my witnesses in Jerusalem, and in all Judea and Samaria, and to the ends of the earth" (Acts 1:8 NIV).

Where are the boundaries established by Christ? Obviously there are none. There may be boundaries established by government and culture—the early church faced these—but none should be imposed by the church itself.

A New Era

In his book *The Once and Future Church: Reinventing the Congregation for a New Mission Frontier*, Loren Mead places within the context of church history the increasing establishment of boundaries for American Christians. He points out that the early Christian church consisted of faithful Christians huddling together (congregating) for worship, prayer, and mutual support amid a hostile and antagonistic external environment.

But they were called upon to go into that hostile world with the

Gospel of Jesus Christ. That was their mission. They did so, sometimes at the expense of their very lives. The boundary between their safe and supportive community of faith and the hostile world was, literally, the walls of the places in which they met. The mission field was right outside the door. Mead calls this the "Apostolic Paradigm."

That all began to change when the Emperor Constantine made Christianity the official religion of the Roman Empire. Nations were by law "Christian," and open hostility toward the church was eliminated from the environment. The boundaries for the faithful Christians were now extended to the very boundaries of the empire. Anyone born within the borders of Italy, France, Germany, Britain, or any of the other western European nations, was immediately assumed to be Christian. No longer did individual believers go into a mission field, except for those few professionals trained and sent by the church to lands beyond the boundaries of the empire, to places like India, China, and Africa. Mead calls this the "Christendom Paradigm." It was during the Christendom period that a hierarchical structure developed in the Christian church. The kleros (clergy) became the ones who ministered, and the laos (laity) became those to whom they ministered. Martin Luther and other Reformers tried to restore the church to a "priesthood of all believers," but the institution was so firmly planted that there has been little change.

The Christendom Paradigm, however, has been changing as our nation becomes more multicultural and "secular." No longer does the Christian church institution exert as much influence in our society as it did one hundred years ago. No longer is the mission field beyond the boundaries of the empire. Once more the mission field is literally appearing outside the doors of our church buildings in an environment that is frequently indifferent, occasionally hostile and only sometimes supportive of the Gospel of Jesus Christ. Mead says we are returning to a time somewhat similar to that of the Apostolic age, a time that requires a new paradigm, the nature of which is not yet fully discernible.

If Mead is correct in his analysis, and I firmly believe he is, then the role of the laity must make a gigantic shift away from that of the dying Christendom model. No longer can the laity be passive members of congregations while their clergy do the missionary work, both here and in far-off lands. No longer are the roles of the laity simply to attend worship services regularly and to support the congregation with their time and their pocketbooks. Increasingly, the full mission of the church is now being given to the laity, who must regularly cross the boundaries beween congregation and world. Mead asserts, ". . . the boundary between the congregation and the world becomes more important than it has been for 1,600 years."[5] Suddenly, Jesus' instruction, "Go into all the world and preach the good news to all creation" (Mark 16:15 NIV), takes on new meaning. Because the boundary is now the perimeter of a congregation, "the world" and "all creation" includes our workplaces, our families, neighborhoods, cities, states, nations, and the globe.

But how will a people raised to think that the church's mission field was in China or Africa or India learn to see that the mission field is at General Motors, K-Mart, the state university, the school board, town hall, Washington, D.C., on a bus, at a picnic, with one's family, at a class reunion, and on and on? And how will they be trained and supported for their missions? Ah, there's the rub. Most of us, laypeople and clergy alike, don't know. We know how to bring people into ministries of the congregation—teaching, singing, ushering, serving on boards and committees—and we know how to train them and, it is to be hoped, support them. But we don't know how to send people out beyond the boundaries of the congregation to minister in and to the world. Clergy have been and continue to be trained in seminaries that were developed under the Christendom model of the church. Only a few of them are beginning to catch a glimpse of a changing mission.

Denominations flourished in times when missions fields were in distant lands. Today, with dwindling church memberships, plummeting financial support, and a rapidly aging laity, denominations struggle to reverse the frightening trends they face. Still, their publishing houses churn out educational materials that are largely irrelevant for Christians whose mission field is right outside the doors of the local church. Meanwhile, local judicatories are increasingly providing hospice care as more and more small congregations slowly die.

In short, survival is the driving force in the mainline denominations. In such an environment, where will the leadership come from? Where will the resources come from? And where will the courage come from to affirm, equip, and support the laity for Christian ministry in and to the world about them?

Ministry in Daily Life

Over the past forty years, a movement powered primarily by laypeople
has slowly been developing within the Christian church in America.
Known originally as "lay ministry," then "ministry of the laity," and
more recently, "ministry in daily life," the movement has permeated all
American denominations to some degree. In some instances, the language has found its way into the governing documents of major denominations.

Here and there one catches a glimpse of a pastor who has the vision
of an empowered laity and the courage to try dramatic steps to bring
about change. Davida Foy Crabtree's vision of a mobilized laity led her
to bring her congregational leadership into an intense study of the role
of its members in the world. The result was dramatic restructuring of
Colchester Federated Church, so that its focus would be on sending out
its people in ministry rather than confining them to congregational ministries. Her book, *The Empowering Church: How One Congregation
Supports Lay People's Ministries in the World*, has been quoted widely
for its account of a dramatic structural change in a congregation. But,
given the pressures cited above, few pastors are indeed willing to take
the gamble Pastor Crabtree did. The Ministry in Daily Life movement
continues to be powered largely by laypeople who take seriously Christ's
admonition to "go into all the world."

What can congregations do to help their members as they cross the
boundary lines between church and world to carry out their ministries in
daily life? This is the question I am most frequently asked by laity and
clergy as I conduct seminars on Ministry in Daily Life. Whenever I do
a workshop called "The Congregation as an Equipping Center," there is
furious note taking as I reel off the "how tos" of it all. It is because of
the obvious interest and need for examples of growing numbers of Christians who carry out Ministry in Daily Life that this book has been written. Most of the examples in this book have come from the experience
of my own congregation, the Lutheran Church of the Holy Spirit in
Emmaus, Pennsylvania. I have picked up some other how tos from observations of other congregations.

Before getting into the meat of the book, I have good news for
pastors who support the principle of every member in ministry but who
are afraid to encourage it for fear that there will be less support for the

survival needs of the congregation: I have never encountered a congregation whose people were engaged in Ministry in Daily Life that was not also a thriving congregation. Never. Not once in over twenty years of working with congregations. The reason is simple: As members seek to carry out their ministries in daily life, they always return to their churches, the places for recharging their spiritual batteries. Through Word and Sacrament, education, and support groups, members of a congregation are renewed for weekday ministry in the world.

The book deals with three crucial needs for ministry in daily life: Christians must be affirmed for their ministries, equipped to better carry them out, and supported in various ways by the congregation.

CHAPTER 2

Defining Ministry

And she arose and ministered unto them. (Matthew 8:15 KJV)

"Bill, I don't understand why you people are pushing ministry in daily life so much," he said. "I understand the theory completely and I support it. I frequently refer to it in my sermons, and we even have a 'Laity Recognition Sunday' once a year when our lay leaders conduct the full service, including preaching the sermon. What's the big deal?"

So said an experienced pastor of a five hundred-member congregation at a workshop I was conducting for clergy. I have heard virtually the same thing from many other clergy. And I am convinced that these pastors sincerely think they do understand the "theory" of ministry in daily life and sincerely believe that what they are doing is equipping members for their ministries in the world.

The belief of many clergy is that lay ministry in the parish is the model for lay ministry in the world. Another pastor put it this way: "I demonstrate to my people the importance of their ministry by having them assist with the liturgy regularly, visit our sick and shut-ins, teach in our Sunday school, actively serve on our committees and church council, and support each other in these ministries. This is how they learn to carry out Christian ministry during the week." In short, this pastor believes that if the Word is rightly preached each Sunday and the Sacraments rightly administered, and if the people are active in the work of the church, then they automatically will know "how to" carry out their daily life ministries.

Nice theory. The only trouble is that it doesn't work. The reason should be obvious. The environment within the boundaries of the congregation is warm and accepting, and there are tried and true ways of doing lay ministry there. On the other hand, the environment beyond the boundaries of the congregation is cool, sometimes cold, to the Christian faith, and most churches do not begin to know what ministry in daily life looks like beyond those boundaries

Ministry in Daily Life

The prolific Quaker writer Elton Trueblood once wrote that the term "Christian minister" is a redundancy because, by its very nature, to be a Christian is to be in ministry, that is, in service to others. The great reformers spoke of a "priesthood of all believers" or "the priesthood of the baptized." The role of a priest, of course, is to represent God to the people and to pray to God on behalf of the people. The priest is the channel for God's action in the world. The reformers were not simply creating this principle out of thin air. The universal priesthood is biblical; both the Old and New Testament make reference to it. Perhaps the most familiar verse is 1 Peter 2:9: "But you are a chosen race, a royal priesthood, a holy nation, God's own people, in order that you may proclaim the mighty acts of him who called you out of darkness into his marvelous light." The priestly role of all the people shows up as early as Exodus 19:4-6 ("You shall be for me a priestly kingdom").

Some other references are Isaiah 61:6 ("but you shall be called priests of the Lord, you shall be named ministers of our God"), and Revelation 1:6 (". . . and made us to be a kingdom, priests serving his God and Father"). Because the word "priest" has a clearly ecclesiastical connotation, the word "minister" is more comfortable for laypeople today. The verb "to minister" means to serve, to act as an agent, or to give help. The Christian, acting as an agent of God, serves in and to the world.

Although there is theological agreement on the theoretical validity of the priesthood of all believers and the universal ministry, in practice our denominations have difficulty with that concept. Are the laity *really* ministers? If so, are not the ordained ministers of a higher order? I was a firsthand witness to this struggle within the Lutheran community. When the Lutheran Church in America, the American Lutheran Church, and the Association of the Evangelical Lutheran Churches came together in the mid-1980s to form a new Lutheran Church, I was a member of the seventy-person Commission for a New Lutheran Church. The topic of ministry was an early and ongoing struggle.

The differing views of ministry were characterized by some as the difference between a three-story house and a ranch house. The three-story-house people saw the laity on the first floor, the clergy on the second floor, and the bishops on the third floor; they saw ministry as hierarchical. Accordingly, it was difficult for them to use the term "minister" for both lay and clergy persons. The ranch-house people saw ministry more in terms of function, with laity in one room, clergy in another room, and bishops in a third room. There were no "higher" forms of ministry, just different functions. In an effort to reach a compromise, some suggested that the laity have a "general ministry" and the clergy have a "specific ministry." Others (both clergy and laity) argued that lay people also have "specific" ministries in the world and that the terms "general" and "specific" still imply a hierarchical structure.

The Lutherans debated for months and finally decided on the following first paragraph for the chapter on ministry in the constitution:

> This church affirms the Universal Priesthood of all its baptized members. In its function and its structure this church commits itself to the equipping and supporting of all its members for their ministries in the world and in this church. It is within this context of ministry that this church calls or appoints some of its baptized members for specific ministries in this church.[6]

The statement says that all the baptized have ministries in the world and *in this church* (meaning the Evangelical Lutheran Church in America). It also recognizes that in this church some are called for specific ministries. Because the Evangelical Lutheran Church in America is a hierarchical structure, it would be correct to say that some of the members (clergy and lay professionals) are called to specific ministries *in this church*. But *in the world, all* baptized members have the same type of ministry. It was a solution that satisfied the three-story people who were focusing on ministry in the church and the ranch house people who were focusing on ministry in the world.

The reformers also claimed that it was in our baptism that God "called" us into the priesthood or, in today's terms, the ministry. Christians have all been "called" into a universal ministry. Paul frequently uses the word "call" in his letters. For example, in his first letter to the church at Corinth, Paul writes, "each one must order his life according to the gift the Lord has granted him and in his condition when God called him" (1 Cor. 7:17 NEB). To the church at Ephesus, he wrote, "I entreat you then . . . as God has called you, live up to your calling" (Eph. 4:1 NEB) We respond to that call in a variety of ways and in a variety of places.

The Arenas of Ministry

We have found it useful at Holy Spirit Church to speak of four arenas of ministry: occupation, family, community, and church. We say that one's occupation is whatever one primarily does with one's time at any given point in life. A paid job is an occupation. But so, too, is the unpaid job of homemaker and parent. Being a student is an occupation, and we try to drive home that point with our youth. They are not simply preparing for an occupation; they are *already* in an occupation and have a ministry there. A person who is out of work has an occupation—that of seeking a job. The group with whom we have the hardest sell is the retired. Retired people have been conditioned to feel that when the paid job is over and the children have left home, there no longer is an occupation. Being a gardener, a traveler, a book reader, a community volunteer are all occupations for those who classify themselves as retired. In all these occupations, there is a call to ministry.

The arena of family is a second place to which Christians have been called to ministry. We define "family" as not only the immediate, nuclear family but as all those with whom we have an ongoing relationship. Aunts, uncles, nieces, nephews, cousins, grandparents, in-laws are all part of one's family. We also include a foreign exchange student, a refugee family we have sponsored, a widowed friend who lives alone, a female ex-offender, and members of our Koinonia group. We call this our extended family.

The third arena, that of community, encompasses one's neighborhood, town, state, nation, and world. We minister by the volunteer roles we play in these various communities. The PTA, school board, volunteer fire department, United Way, Boy Scouts, Meals on Wheels, Rotary Club, and a multitude of other groups are the settings for local community ministries. Ministry in community means being an informed voter in local, state, and national elections. It means writing letters to our elected officials and to the editor of a newspaper or magazine on issues of concern to society.

The fourth arena, ministry in the church, involves our local congregation or parish, our regional church structure, our denomination, and the Christian church at large. It includes serving on committees, assisting in worship services, being generous in our giving, supporting our staff, and inviting others into our fellowship. It can extend to serving on committees of local, state, or national councils of churches, as well as local and national denominational expressions.

As Christians, we have one calling, the universal calling to ministry. We can answer that call with simultaneous ministries in the four arenas cited above. For example, I have a ministry in my job as a management consultant. At the same time, I have a ministry to my wife, children, grandchildren, and extended family members. I also concurrently have a ministry as a neighbor to the Clark family; as a member of the Lehigh Valley Housing Authority; as an informed citizen who votes in town, state, and national elections; and as one who cares about global peace, hunger, and the environment. Finally, I am also called into ministry as an active member of Holy Spirit Church, as a member of the National Church Council of the Evangelical Lutheran Church in America, and as president of the international, ecumenical Coalition for Ministry in Daily Life. I have many ministries in many places. On any given day, I may be spending much of my time and energy on one or two of them, but over the period of several months, I do minister in all of them.

It may sound as if anything and everything a Christian does is ministry. But that's not quite so. If one acts in a way that is un-Christian or ungodly, it is not ministry. The first chapter of Genesis gives us the yardstick by which to measure. Recall that at the end of each step of creation, "God saw that it was good." On the sixth day of creation, "God created humankind in his image." God gave all of creation to humans along with God's very first commandment: "Be fruitful and multiply, and fill the earth and subdue it; and have dominion over . . . every living thing that moves upon the earth" (Gen. 1:28). To "subdue" the earth means to cultivate it. Then "God saw everything that he had made, and indeed, it was very good" (Gen. 1:31).

The yardstick for defining ministry is whether we, who were created in the image of God, protect and extend God's creation, which is "very good." Actions destructive to God's creation are not ministry. Certainly the peddling of addictive drugs is not ministry. Nor is defrauding people in business. But how about growing tobacco and marketing cigarettes? Or working in a drug store that sells pornographic magazines and greeting cards? It isn't always black and white. Christians must prayerfully consider some of the gray areas and then decide for themselves. But largely, it is clear: What protects and extends God's creation is ministry.

Styles of Ministry

Styles of ministry are diverse. If we define ministry as those actions that preserve and extend the creation God entrusted to humans, styles of ministry include the following:

1. Words and Deeds. Most of my Christian friends define their ministries exclusively by the deeds they do—and don't do. "I try to be kind to all people," or "I never tell a lie," or "I practice the golden rule." These actions are indeed ministry, but if we do not see that there is also a ministry of words, we have some growing to do.

"I don't need to talk about my faith," say many Christians, "because people will know I'm a Christian by my deeds." To this, Trueblood had a good rejoinder. He said many times, "Anyone who says he or she can be seen as a Christian by others purely through their deeds is insufferably self-righteous. No one is that good. There are times when we must speak about our faith."

Jesus ministered by both word and deed, sometimes purely by word, sometimes purely by deed. Frequently, his deeds of mercy were followed with words about the kingdom of God. Should not the followers of Jesus do the same?

2. To Individuals and Organizations. It is easy to see that on a one-to-one basis, we carry out ministry. We visit a sick person, tutor a child, provide hospitality to a stranger, act as a Big Brother or Big Sister. The list can go on and on.

We also serve God's creation through ministry to organizations. The most obvious example is our service to our congregation. But we also minister to our school system by serving on the school board, as difficult as that can sometimes be. We minister to our government by

voting and taking an active part in political issues. Sometimes that can
make us very unpopular. When my wife Judy and I helped organize a
fair housing committee for the Main Line communities of Philadelphia,
many of the people in our congregation were upset. When we marched
in Washington, D.C., in protest of the Vietnam War, many of my corporate associates were scandalized. But in both cases, we were trying to
redirect our government in the cause of justice and peace. We were in
ministry to our society.

   We can also minister to our society when we challenge false values.
Today, consumerism and materialism are running rampant in our society.
As Christians, we should be challenging these values by having a lifestyle that demonstrates we reject them. But this is a difficult one for most
of us. We like our expensive cars, big homes, fashionable clothing, and
costly vacations. Today's Christians' lifestyles are a far cry from the
countercultural life of Jesus or the simple life of the early church. We
are called to challenge the false values, the false gods of our time.

   Jesus is well remembered for his one-to-one ministry. He healed the
sick, restored sight to the blind, and became friends with those whom
society scorned. But he also ministered to groups. He fed the multitude
and preached the good news. And he ministered to the religious organization of his day by exposing the hypocrisy of its leaders and the distor-
tions of its legalism.

   3. Direct and Indirect. We minister to others directly when we are
in a face-to-face situation with them. We minister indirectly when we
go through some third party. For example, when we give money and
time to our local United Way, we never know precisely who will benefit
from our giving. Only the United Way knows of our gift. When we give
blood at the blood bank, the recipient will probably be unknown to us.
Only the blood bank knows of our action.

   Most of Jesus' ministry was direct. But when he sent out the Twelve
to "cure the sick, raise the dead, cleanse the lepers, cast out demons"
(Matt. 10:8), his ministry was done indirectly.

   4. Overt and Covert. Again, our direct, one-to-one ministry is obviously overt. But there are times when we don't want anyone to know
of our ministry. A covert, anonymous gift to a needy friend can save that
person embarrassment.

   Jesus' ministry was almost exclusively overt, although occasionally
he wanted to be covert. For example, he asked the leper whom he healed

not to tell anyone (Mark 1:43-44). Jesus provides many good examples
of how we can do ministry in the twenty-first century—in both word and
deed.

Intentionality

Many times it has been said that the church should go into the world.
The fact is that the church already *is* in the world. It is present in the
many Christians who daily labor in factories and farms, who are faithful
husbands and wives, who are caring parents, who uphold society's laws,
and who vote on election day. And they minister to others in acts of
kindness, by caring for our environment, in love for family, in honesty,
and in many other ways. They minister when they are the bearers of
hope in a hopeless society.

The problem is that many Christians do not see themselves in ministry and do not sense that they have been called by God into ministry.
They go through life totally missing the glorious knowledge that they
live in a partnership with God and, in certain instances, are the channel
for God's action in their world. They worship in their churches on Sunday and sense God's presence there but fail to sense God's presence in
their weekday world.

Craig Mucher is an industrial chemist. Sandy Taylor is a technical
writer. And Dave Fishburn is a retired truck driver. But it is obvious
that all of them are ministers, for they speak freely of being called by
God to give witness to the Gospel by what they say and do in their daily
lives. And each one is vibrantly alive in the faith. Our work life is im-
measurably enriched when we know that we have been called to it by a
God who cares about us and is present with us. Equally important, our
faith life takes on new meaning when we know we are empowered for
Ministry in Daily Life.

At the Lutheran Church of the Holy Spirit, we are trying hard to help
our people understand that they have been called into ministry at baptism
and that their ministry is in those places and situations where God has
already placed them. We try to affirm them in that ministry, equip them
to be more intentional about it, and find ways to support them in it. Considering all the boundaries we face between church and world and considering all the years we were told that ministry happened only in the

church, this affirming, equipping, and supporting does not come easily.
But we are light years away from those annual lay recognition Sundays
of bygone years.

However valuable the participation of laymen in public worship may
be, it must be clearly understood that such is never the lay member's
chief ministry. In the nature of the case, his chief witness must be
given outside the place of worship, for the vineyard, where laborers
are needed, is not located in the church building. It is located most
often in the factories and offices and clubs.[7]

CHAPTER 3

Affirming the People

But, you are a chosen race, a royal priesthood, a holy nation, God's own people . . . who called you out of darkness into his marvelous light. (1 Peter 2:9)

"Bill, the reception desk just phoned and there's a . . . ah . . . minister down in the lobby who wants to see you," my secretary said in a somewhat uncertain voice.

"Oh, yes," I replied. "It's my pastor, Tom Reinsel. Have them bring him up."

Affirming People in the Workplace

Tom was the second pastor to serve our congregation. He arrived shortly after we joined Holy Spirit Church, and it was with him that Ministry in Daily Life began to take shape among us. Tom had come to my office at Bethlehem Steel to learn more about my job there. His visit was the result of a breakfast conversation we had several weeks earlier in which I pointed out that pastors make home visits but not workplace visits. I told him I thought that if pastors made some workplace visits, they would learn more about the lives of their members and would most certainly affirm the ministry of those members in the workplace. He agreed to try a visit to my office as an experiment.

While I was awaiting his arrival, I wondered how he would be dressed. He was usually very informal in his dress, wearing his clerical collar only for hospital visits or special occasions. In a few moments Tom appeared with the escort at the doorway to the large secretarial area outside my office. He was dressed in his brown suit with the white clerical collar. This was to be a special occasion.

As my secretary met him at the door and escorted him past the desks of a number of other secretaries to my office, I noticed that the eyes of everyone in the room were glued on him. I can only imagine how the questions flew as I closed the door. What was up? Was the boss in trouble? Was he getting counseling?

We sat down and I began explaining what a manager of sales at Bethlehem Steel does. I kept the phone lines open, and as calls came in from Chicago or Atlanta or San Francisco, I handled them in my normal manner and then explained to Tom what each call was about. He was quite interested and asked many questions. Not once was there a mention of our congregation. The focus was totally on my job.

After about a half hour, he felt it was time to leave. I opened my office door and escorted him past all the secretaries out to the hall where he could catch an elevator. Again, all eyes were on us. When I returned everyone was busily at work—as if nothing unusual had happened. But I knew they were curious. So I told them. "I guess you wonder why my pastor was here," I said to the group. "He was here to learn about my job and the kind of Christian ministry I do here."

I could tell by the blank looks on their faces that they didn't understand. "The boss is a minister?" they had to be thinking. So I continued.

"In our church we teach that all members have their own ministries—in their homes, in their communities, and even in their places of work. While I have never talked 'religion' in the office here, I have tried to carry out my job as a Christian. That's why he was here—to learn about what I do so that he can be supportive of my ministry."

When I next saw Tom, he was very excited about the visit and had already made other appointments to call on people where they worked. Over the next year he must have visited over thirty people at their places of work. In not all cases could he talk with them as they worked, but he did have lunch with them and occasionally took his own brown-bag lunch along.

Reflecting upon it a year later, Tom said that the visits gave him a much clearer sense of what our people were up against as they tried to connect Sunday worship with their weekday world. "And man," he chuckled, "do I have sermon material now!"

He did have new material, and his sermons began to connect clearly with the so-called real world of our people. As for me, Tom's visit was a great affirmation of my ministry at Bethlehem Steel. Up to that point, I had had an intellectual sense of being in ministry in my job, but his visit validated that sense for me because for the first time "my church" had come into "my world." Moreover, his visit gave me an opening to explain to a number of people in my department that I felt I had a Christian ministry in my job. Knowing how well our grapevine worked, I was certain that my explanation of the pastor's visit was known throughout our department—and beyond—within a few days.

A few years later Tom moved on to a new congregation and Pastor Al arrived. He continued to visit places of work. In a few instances where several members worked for the same company, he began monthly visits with the group. One major company even gave him a private lunch room where he could meet with those employees who were members of our congregation. He is convinced that having a firsthand knowledge of the work situations of many of our members is essential for his preaching. Neither Tom nor Al could visit the workplaces of all our members, so they never advertised that they were doing the visits. They visited quietly and with the intention of affirming those members who seemed to understand that they had a ministry in daily life.

It is absolutely essential that the daily ministries of all Christians be affirmed. But such affirmation doesn't come easily, because the church, like any other institution, has a demonic nature to it. Demons try to possess people, to own them. A demonic organization is one that tries to take over the lives of its members. As only too many people have found, their jobs can easily possess them, taking countless hours out of their lives and still seeking more. So it can be with our churches. There is no limit to the number of hours of volunteer service that our churches will gladly accept from us.

But the Christian church *claims* to be an institution that gathers people on Sunday and then scatters them into the world for Christian service the rest of the week. The church says it gathers people for worship, study, and fellowship presumably *so that* they can be effective in their worldly ministry. The church asserts that it is not an end in itself but a means to an end. Yet an examination of a typical congregation's newsletter suggests, by what the newsletter prints and what it omits, that "churchy" activity is an end in itself.

The only way to overcome the demonic nature of the congregation is to affirm in every way possible that ministry in and to the world is fundamental to the faith. At Holy Spirit Church, we seek to affirm people on both sides of the boundaries that separate the congregation from the world. The pastor's visit to the place of occupation is a good example of how the church can be affirming in the workplace. Workplace support groups are another way to affirm ministry. By what it says and does, a congregation must help people sense God's presence in the workplace as clearly as in the worship place. Here are some ways we try to develop that spirituality.

Affirming People in Worship

Worship is at the core of a congregation's life. That means that if people are to be affirmed in their daily life ministries, ways must be found to do it within the context of a worship service.

Preaching

Preaching, of course, is an obvious place for linking faith and daily life. Reinhold Niebuhr said that every sermon should be given with the newspaper in one hand and the Bible in the other. I really agree with that. People come to Sunday worship with many things on their minds, some personal and some societal. There are so many news stories confronting us each day that any preacher can easily make a connection between one of them and the lessons appointed for the day. I much prefer to hear a sermon begin with a daily life issue and then go on to show how it is addressed by the Word of God as revealed in the lessons of the day. It is much less effective to my ears to begin with an exegesis of the lessons of the day and then to make a connection with a daily life issue.

Why do I prefer that? Because that's the order in which events play out in our daily lives. On any given day, we are faced with a variety of problems or issues. As we try to deal with them, we should get in the habit of mentally sifting through our biblical and theological knowledge to make a helpful connection. When the preacher uses this order in a sermon, individuals are encouraged to follow the same procedure in daily life situations. We also see the importance of enlarging our personal store of biblical knowledge, which for many is woefully small.

Apart from using news items, another way to make sure the sermon relates to the daily life issues of members is through a pre-sermon focus group. Three or four members of the congregation are asked to read the lessons for the coming Sunday and then to meet with the pastor to share the daily life issues that come to their minds when they read the lessons. The difficulty is trying to schedule a regular meeting time. (The last time we had pre-sermon focus groups at Holy Spirit, we ran into so many problems scheduling three preaching pastors and four members that we abandoned the group after about three months. I felt something was lost by not continuing the groups.)

Services of Affirmation

In January each year, we elect new members to our congregation council. At one of the worship services in late January, our pastor installs the new council members in a special rite before the altar. As a part of the rite, the pastor asks members of the congregation if they will pray for these new council members and support them in their service to the congregation. "We will," responds the congregation.

In a similar manner, many congregations also install and affirm their Sunday school teachers in September, their vacation church school teachers in July, and other special volunteers from time to time—always within the context of a worship service. Affirming people for their ministries in the congregation is common.

Is it possible also to affirm our members who are in ministry beyond the boundaries of our congregation? The answer is yes, and at Holy Spirit Church we do. Once in the spring and once in the fall, we have a service of affirmation of ministry in which we recognize various occupational categories. "Occupation" is not synonymous with "work" at Holy Spirit. Occupation is that activity that most "occupies" a member's time. For many, occupation means a paid job. But homemakers, retirees, students, and community volunteers are also "occupied." We have identified eight occupational groupings, each broad in scope. For example, the education group includes teachers, administrators, students, bus drivers, food servers, school board members, and the like. Other occupational groups are health care, business and industry, homemaking, science and technology, retirement, public service, and the arts.

Take, for example, the time we affirmed peoples' ministry in science and technology. Using our parish directory, we were able to identify sixty-three people in the congregation who worked in this broad area. We then wrote to each of them, inviting them to attend a series, "TechnoMania," at our Center for Faith and Life and also to be present on a specified Sunday for a service of affirmation for people who work in science and technology. In the four-week series, members examined how the rapid increases in computer technology are affecting our society. We had a different topic and discussion leader each week. Scientists and technicians openly shared concerns.

Then at our 11:00 A.M. worship service on the specified day, members who work in science and technology were invited to come forward for a short rite of affirmation in which the pastor proclaimed that they are sent out by the congregation of Holy Spirit to be our ministers in the field of science and technology. Not everyone felt comfortable participating in this rite, but about twenty people did come forward. The congregation was asked to pray for them and support them in these ministries beyond the boundaries. The congregation responded with a firm "We will!"

Some congregations use a "rite of affirmation." Others use the word "commissioning," although in some denominations, "commissioning" presents a problem due to ecclesiastical practices. The phrase "sending out" also works well. The point is that if we affirm or commission people for their ministries in the congregation, we certainly need to find similar ways to recognize ministries in the world.

In the many congregations to which we have belonged as we have moved around the country, I have been publicly affirmed in my congregational ministries dozens of times. It has become commonplace. But the first time my ministry in the field of business was affirmed, within the context of a worship service at Holy Spirit, was very special.

Prayers in the Worship Service

Laypeople who assist in all our worship services are encouraged to write their own prayers. These prayers are always directly related to daily life events; they are often very moving. The pastors do not review these prayers prior to the worship service. They come directly from the hearts of our members. There may be prayers for those who recently lost their jobs at Bethlehem Steel, the schoolteacher who was just killed in an automobile accident, the crisis in the Middle East, the earthquake in Japan, the forthcoming election. The prayers also include thanks and intercession for the needs of the congregation, but they invariably start with the needs of the world. They may not always be in the most flowery language and, occasionally, the theology is a "bit un-Lutheran," but they are the honest prayers of our people.

Reaffirmation of Baptism

It has been said that at baptism all God's people are ordained for Christian ministry. There can be various ways to remember or reaffirm our baptisms during a worship service. The Evangelical Lutheran Church in America has a special rite for reaffirmation of baptism. If your denomination does not, why not write one? This rite is not a second baptism; it is a reminder of our first baptism.

Recognizing National Holidays

National holidays offer wonderful opportunities to connect faith and daily life within the context of a congregational worship service. Recognition of them in the worship service is another way to bring the weekday world into the Sunday world. We frequently use the Sunday after Labor Day as an opportunity to lift up the ministries of our people in the places of work. (We find that the Sunday *of* Labor Day weekend has poor worship attendance; thus we focus on the Sunday *after*.) This Sunday provides the preacher with an opportunity to focus on a "spirituality of work," a term coined by Pope John Paul II. But this is only one way to highlight the faith-work connection. In some years, we have asked people to come to worship dressed as they dress for work. People can wear their uniforms or work clothes. In our congregation not too much changes because many of our members are business and professional people who dress essentially the same on Sunday as on Monday. In blue collar congregations, however, the work dress is much more interesting.

Roberta Longsworth, our first director of lay ministries, once suggested that we ask people to bring to worship a symbol of their daily work. During the period normally given to an offering, we asked people to come forward and lay their work symbols on a large table in front of the altar. In our congregation, we see a greater variety of work symbols than ways of dressing for work. People will bring laptop computers, pieces of chalk, stethoscopes, cellular phones, date books, carpentry tools, cake pans, and so forth. In the context of an offering during the worship service, the occupational symbols are effective.

Election day is the time to emphasize our ministry in the community. We urge people to vote. Many people don't realize that voting is a ministry to the community. (Incidentally, voter registration cards are given to every adult who joins the congregation. We believe a high percentage of our members are registered voters and that they do vote on election days.)

Other national holidays such as Presidents' Day, Memorial Day, and Independence Day offer opportunities to stress ministry in community. The Sunday closest to Martin Luther King Jr.'s birthday is an opportune time to focus on how our community ministry must work to eliminate bigotry and discrimination. For Mothers' Day and Fathers' Day, we try to stress the ministry of parenting, although because a number of the children in our congregation have only one parent living with them, we are careful not to give the impression that single-parent families are inferior.

Our pastors have been encouraged to introduce the Sunday worship service by citing *both* the church day and the national or community day or event. For example, "Today is the sixth Sunday after Pentecost and the Sunday before Independence Day" or "Today is the second Sunday after Easter and the Sunday following the tragic fire in the Sunset nursing home." Our pastors are not too keen on this, but we know that people come to worship with their minds on secular events. Again, the purpose is to connect faith with daily life.

Our Sunday morning schedule allows parents and children to attend worship together. It is our hope that the affirmation of ministry within the worship service is educating our children also.

Banners and Bulletins

Many congregations have banners in their worship areas. Here again is a chance to affirm ministry in daily life in a wide variety of ways. Our favorite banner at Holy Spirit Church is a bright red one with a huge white cross on it. A huge black thumbprint is superimposed on the cross. That's it. No words. But the meaning is simple: Your ministry is as individual as your thumbprint. There are countless ways to communicate ministry in daily life through banners.

Worship bulletins can also proclaim the faith-life connection. Today the bulletins of many congregations list the pastors by name but also indicate that "the ministers" are all the members of the congregation. On our worship bulletin appear the words, "The Holy Spirit Empowers Us for Ministry in Daily Life." That sentence also appears on all our stationery, envelopes, coffee cups—everywhere! The final sentence on the worship bulletins of some congregations is, "The worship is over; let the service begin."

Other Tools for Affirming Ministry

The Parish Directory

Our parish directory, which is reissued each year, carries the name, address, phone number, *and* occupation of every baptized member of the congregation. Remember that we define occupation as that activity in which we spend most of our time each day. For many, occupation is a paid job and we list the type of job and employer. For example, Linda Krentz is listed as a professor of biochemistry at Lehigh University, and Kim Kroll is listed as a scientist at Rodale Institute. A number of women are listed as homemakers. Children and youth are listed by their grade in school or college. We still have a bit of a problem with retired people, most of whom want to be listed simply as "retired." We are trying to get them to think in terms of what occupies their time, and we encourage such entries as "driver for Meals on Wheels," "hospital volunteer" "gardener," or "traveler." The point is that we all are called into ministry in whatever occupation we find ourselves, provided, of course, that it preserves and honors God's creation. But most of our older retirees don't see themselves as having a ministry, so we list them as they wish.

"What about the unemployed?" someone always asks. Again, we honor the wishes of each member. But, if someone is without a paid job at the time the directory is being revised, we suggest they simply be listed using a generic form such as "scientist," "factory worker," or "secretary."

Our office staff, by their own admission, continually complain about the need to show occupations because there is so much more work entailed in updating each issue. In response we refer them to the paragraph in the front of the directory:

> This directory is one way in which The Lutheran Church of the Holy Spirit affirms the ministry in daily life of each of our members. As Lutherans we believe that every baptized person has been called by God for various ministries in his or her daily life. Our arenas of ministry are in our families, our communities, our church and our occupations. Our "occupation" is that daily activity that occupies most of our time. A worker in a paid job, a homemaker, a student and an active retired person are all in occupations and, in the eyes of God, they are of equal worth. God accepts us not as the world might judge the "Importance" of our occupation but simply by our faith.
>
> But because many of us find it difficult to see any ministry in our occupation and because, as a congregation, we truly believe that "The Holy Spirit Empowers Us for Ministry in Daily Life," we make this special effort to affirm the occupational ministries of all our members by listing them in this directory.

Having people's occupations listed in our directory not only affirms their ministries but also helps greatly to locate resource persons for the programs of the Center for Faith and Life, as will be seen in the next chapter.

Bulletin Boards

At one of the entrances to our building is a large bulletin board with the heading, "Our People in Ministry." On it are tacked newspaper articles in which the name of one of our members is mentioned. The name is highlighted in yellow. Articles may be about job promotions, school honor rolls, community service activities, school athletic achievements, letters to the editor, and so forth. Our director of member ministries carefully goes through the daily Allentown *Morning Call* and the weekly *East Penn Press* to locate such articles. It is a painstaking job, but each time a person's name appears on that bulletin board, that person's arena of ministry is affirmed.

(I'm frequently asked by some teaser if items from the police reports are included. The answer is no. Running afoul of the law is not preserv- ing or honoring God's creation and, therefore, is not Christian ministry. That's the theological answer. The wishful-thinking answer is that all our members are *so* good that their names *never* appear in police reports. The theological answer is possibly more accurate.)

A number of years ago, a former director of Christian education, "B.J." Weigang, decided to do a major display on our youth in ministry. After explaining what was meant by ministry in daily life, B.J. asked to photograph each youth in a place where they do ministry. She allowed them to choose the location. Most of them selected the school class- room, but some picked a part-time job, such as lawn mowing or baby- sitting, while others selected volunteer work, such as helping at a nearby nursing home. Over a period of weeks, B.J. took an instant photo of each one. Then, one Sunday morning, we were all surprised to see all the photos mounted on a large concrete block wall with huge cut-out letters arched over the top saying "Our Youth in Ministry." It was a real eye- catcher for everyone in the congregation. Of even greater importance was the way in which it affirmed that youth are in ministry also. B.J. reported that several of the youth were very moved that someone from the church would take the time to come and photograph them.

Newsletters

Like most congregations, we have a newsletter. It is mailed to every member home twice a month. It used to be devoted entirely to the inner activities of our congregation. The front page consisted of a "sermon- ette" written by one of our staff. Inside would be articles written by our director of music, our parish nurse, our youth advisors, and others. There

were many thank-you columns from committee chairpersons and announcements of coming events. Members of our staff pointed out that it
seemed a bit contradictory that a congregation with such a strong emphasis on Ministry in Daily Life had as its chief means of communication a
newsletter with an almost exclusively inward focus.

A communication consultant was called in and, after doing several
focus groups, the consultants reported that the newsletter was generally
not read cover to cover. The front page "sermonettes" were almost never
read (much to the shock of our staff). The thank-you lists were not read,
except by those who expected to be on the list. There also were negative
reactions to the thank-you lists by people who were overlooked.

We decided to scrap the old newsletter and start from scratch. The
present newsletter has a different title and a different color. We have a
new format that features a page-one article with a photo about the ministry of a member of our congregation. We invite members to write their
own profiles or, more often, we interview them and do the article about
them. The inside pages of the newsletter still carry brief announcements
about forthcoming events but also feature items related to ministry in
daily life. The change has produced a dramatic turn around in reader-
ship. Now the page-one article *is* read, as is the rest of the newsletter.

If a congregation is truly dedicated to affirming, equipping, and supporting its members for daily ministry in the world, it must be certain
that it does not send contradictory messages to the people. Our newsletter used to have an entirely inward focus. Now it looks outward to our
ministries in daily life.

Signs

We are not big on signs, but I have been in churches where signs are
thought provoking. One congregation has placed the sign, "Servant's
Entrance," above every exterior door but on the *inside*, so that as wor-
shippers exit the church building, they are reminded that they are entering the field of servanthood. Similarly, another congregation has placed
the sign, "The Worship is over, let the Service begin," above the exits
from their worship area. The same message is printed at the end of their
Sunday bulletin. (Perhaps, in the spirit of this book, we should have a
sign above the exits to our building saying, "You are entering the mission field." I think I'll suggest it.)

Collected Faith Stories

Beverly Larson, director of lay ministries at Northridge Lutheran Church in Kalispell, Montana, has produced an excellent congregational booklet we plan to imitate. Over a period of time Bev talked to various members of the congregation about their ministries. She taped some conversations. Other members were willing to write about their ministries or faith stories. She collected all the stories in a booklet with an attractive cover that bears the mission statement of the congregation: "The mission of this congregation is to become a fellowship of Christian believers who touch people's lives as Christ does."

It is a wonderful and moving collection of the witness of some fifty people in the congregation. Seldom do congregations have a way of hearing about the faith convictions and the ministry activities of other members. For it is by learning how our brothers and sisters in the faith express their personal beliefs and carry out their faith in daily life that we can gain inspiration and courage for ourselves. Bev Larson has succeeded admirably in giving us a way to do it.

Recognition Events

Our first director of lay ministries, Roberta Longsworth, and our present director of member ministries, Pam Bonina, had previous professional experience as directors of volunteers for social service agencies. They both knew the importance of thanking volunteers. It has been relatively easy to thank members of the congregation for their ministries in our church, but how can we thank people for their ministries in the world?

Both Roberta and Pam have resorted to periodic recognition dinners for those who have completed congregational ministries; council members, committee members, teachers, and so on. Pam wondered if she could somehow thank these same people for their ministries in the world also. Prior to one dinner, she sent the usual letter of invitation to those whose congregational ministries were to be recognized and included a return postcard on which she asked the invitees to list the ministries they had in the community. She was surprised by the difficulty many people had responding to that request. A number of people assumed that what was wanted was information about church-related volunteerism in the

community. Some wrote that they delivered altar flowers following a
worship service or participated in an Emmaus area ecumenical choir.
Many cards came back blank. Only a few people caught on and sent in
notes about community volunteerism. Pam had to go back and explain
what was wanted before people understood and responded. It was an
example of many people still assuming that the church is interested only
in "church work."

Because many of our members are corporate business and professional people, we have a fairly high turnover of members. Currently, we
are gaining about 120 new adult members each year and are losing about
30, due to corporate downsizing, transfers, and young adults moving out
when they complete college and form families of their own. This turnover presents a bit of a problem for our efforts to affirm people. For example, to ask members to come to worship the Sunday after Labor Day,
dressed as they will for work, is for new members a novel and meaningful means of affirming ministries, but it soon becomes old hat for those
who have done it several times before. So we need to be careful to repeat
some of the affirming activities often enough to pick up our new members but not so often that they become stale for the older members.

It is important to emphasize that everything we do to affirm our
people's ministry in daily life can be done in small, medium, and large
congregations. When our family joined Holy Spirit in 1972, it had fewer
than four hundred baptized members; today it has more than sixteen hundred, and along with member growth has come an increase in staff. But
the ways we affirm ministry are not related to membership size. Whether congregations are large or small, affirming the ministries of the people
is possible and extremely important.

CHAPTER 4

Equipping the People

Now may the God of peace . . . equip you with everything good that you may do his will. (Hebrews 13:20-21 RSV)

"Before we joined Holy Spirit Church, my husband never attended adult education programs in any of the churches in which we were members. At Holy Spirit he never misses one." So said a woman about six months after they joined Holy Spirit.

A new member commented after his fourth breakfast with the Monday Connection, "This is the most exciting thing I have ever been involved with in any church."

"I wish you didn't have two tracks each Sunday morning in the Center for Faith and Life. I never can decide which one to attend!" sighed a long-time member of the congregation.

If we are to do God's will in our daily life ministries, we need to be equipped with practical ways of connecting our Sunday worship and study with the experiences of our daily lives as we cross the boundaries between church and world. Through a variety of educational programs, we work hard at teaching the "how-tos" of Ministry in Daily Life.

In a survey we conducted among participants in our Center for Faith and Life, which meets on Sunday mornings, 92 percent agreed with the statement, "All Christians have been called by God into ministry." At the same time, 66 percent of the group agreed that they "needed more help in making the connections between faith and daily life." In short, understanding the concept of Ministry in Daily Life is not enough. We need to be able to make the connections between Sunday and Monday.

There are a variety of ways to equip members of the congregation to carry their ministries across the boundary lines into occupations, community service, and even families. (Our survey also showed that 22 percent of our people do not feel comfortable talking about their faith with friends and family.) The most logical place to start is with Sunday morning adult education.

Sunday Morning Adult Education

When Judy and I joined Holy Spirit Church, there was virtually no adult education program. The Lutheran Church of the Holy Spirit had been founded in 1961 by a group of families searching for a more stimulating environment than was available in the church they had been attending. The congregation of seventy-nine adults and eleven children struggled to become viable without the services of a full-time pastor. Many families made great leaps of faith to support the young church. The congregation's focus was understandably inward. In the early years adult education was almost exclusively Bible study, taught by the pastor. Bible study, in itself, does not help people very much when they cross the boundaries to Monday. A good Bible teacher will try to introduce practical applications, but such applications often are much too general and sometimes strained. This is not to say we don't need Bible study in adult education. We certainly do, for reasons explained later in this chapter. However, Bible study alone will not adequately equip people for Ministry in Daily Life.

For example, throughout the Bible comes the message of the wonderful grace of God; a grace freely given to the people of God. We do not earn the grace of God; it is a gift of love. Amazing grace! The Bible is clear on this point. When, however, we as God's people leave the church, we perceive a vastly different situation. Virtually everything is based on work and merit. We identify ourselves by what we do, not by whose we are. Our place on the world stage is determined by how well we perform: the grades we get in school, how well we score in sports, the goals we meet in the workplace, the performance of our children, the number of people we manage, our golf handicap or bowling average. And we show the world how well we have performed by the cars we drive, the houses we live in, the clubs to which we belong, and on and on.

While the grace of God is operating in the world, it is very difficult for work-oriented people to feel that grace. In fact, it has been my experience that the most difficult thing for me to do across the boundary line between Sunday and Monday is to explain convincingly the grace of God to a world that worships performance. The two theologies are 180 degrees apart. On the one hand, our weekday world of goals and performance and annual evaluations leads us to a mind set that says we can also earn God's love and acceptance if we are "good enough." On the other hand, our theology of grace says that God already loves and accepts us without any merit of our own. It is because God loves us that we want to do good works. How can we help people to see God's grace in their daily lives? We will never learn how to see God's grace at work in our daily lives simply by studying the Bible. We desperately need help with the how-tos.

When Tom Reinsel came to be pastor of Holy Spirit Church, we began to deal with how to witness in the world without turning people off. We used a new program (no longer available) called *Word and Witness*. It required a two-year commitment to study on a weekday evening with a group of about twelve to fifteen people. We would begin with an intensive period of Bible study and conclude with witnessing skills.

The witnessing segment was based on first listening to the other person, not "telling" him or her. Many people are turned off by enthusiastic Christians who tell them about Jesus without listening to their stories. We were taught how to listen to other people in a way that would let them feel comfortable sharing their life concerns or special problems with us. We called this first stage "your story." Following this intense listening, we were usually able to share life experiences of our own that related to the story of the other. We might discuss the loss of a loved one, concerns about a job, worry over a health problem, concern about children, and so on. We called that stage "my story." At the intersection of "your story" and "my story" could come "God's story," and we would share how God's word was part of "my story" and could be part of yours. It was an effective and exciting program that we repeated a number of times. (There are a number of other study programs that link the Bible with daily life experiences. See the appendix.)

As I began teaching on Sunday mornings at Holy Spirit, I came to the conclusion that most of our denominational adult courses lacked convincing connections between faith and daily life. For a number of years we limped along with about fifteen people regularly in Bible study with the pastor, and ten to fifteen adults working with me on such stand-alone courses as *Monday's Ministers* by Nelvin Vos (no longer in print), or exploring gift identification, effective listening, and some of my own books. But we were reaching only 5 percent of our congregation. We decided to try a new approach: The Center for Faith and Life.

The Center for Faith and Life

We said to ourselves, "Look, because we talk about ministry in occupation, family, community, and church, why not structure a learning center that will offer courses tailored to the needs and concerns in these four arenas?" Initially we asked about forty volunteers to help plan a new approach to adult education. After explaining the four sectors for ministry, we let them self-select into one of four planning groups. We asked each planning committee to design, within the next year, five program series of four Sundays each on their ministry sector, and to secure the resources for presenting these series. "Ask yourselves," we said to the committees, "what things are on the minds of our members in your ministry sector." We asked them to include the faith connection and to plan no more than twenty minutes of lecture and then thirty minutes for discussion. The planning groups would meet only as often as needed to plan their five programs per year. (We did not plan programs for July and August.) Once a month the planning committee chairs would meet with me to coordinate schedules.

We reminded the planners to consider the make-up of our congregation. About 10 percent of our members are 55 and older, a very low percentage for most mainline congregations. Another 20 percent are under 30. That leaves a huge 70 percent of us between 30 and 55, which is a much higher percentage than most mainline congregations. The 1990 U.S. Census report for our postal zone shows a population that is 98.5 percent white with an average family income of $45,538. Our congregation has only one family that is not white, and our average family income is probably a bit higher than the average in our zone. Because we have a high percentage of people in the 30-to-55 age group, many of our families (about 35 percent) are married couples with children still at home. (This is above the community average.) About 8 percent of our households are headed by a single male or female with children at home. We asked our planners to design an education program to meet the needs of all our people but to emphasize the major population groups.

We also determined that every Sunday we would offer a foundational course that would always be taught by a pastor and would include programs on Bible study, Lutheran theology, and the basic concepts of Ministry in Daily Life. We had space available for only three classes per Sunday morning. One would always be foundational. The other two would be four-week series in two of the four ministry sectors—occupation, family, community, or church.

Our First Programs

We got off to a good start in September of our first year. The planning group for Ministry in Family quickly came up with their five programs. Series such as "How to Manage Controversy," "Work and Family," "Family Communications," "Death in the Family," "The 'Sandwich' Family," and "His, Hers, and Ours" (meaning children) were immediately appealing and regularly drew twenty to thirty people.

The Ministry in Occupation group presented programs such as "Christian Ethics and Business," "Jesus as Supervisor," and a whole group of "Ministry in _____" series, such as "Ministry in Education" and "Ministry in Health Care." Additional occupational arenas such as science and technology, public service, homemaking, business, and industry would also be covered. The "Ministry in _____" series always included a worship service of affirmation. As mentioned in the previous chapter, we used the occupational listings in our parish directory to send a special, written invitation to all those members of the congregation who were connected with the particular ministry arena under study.

The Ministry in Community group offered courses such as "Christians with Public Responsibility," "Volunteerism in the Lehigh Valley," "Environmental Stewardship," and "Regional Planning."

The Ministry in Church group dealt with such topics as the proposed social statements of the Evangelical Lutheran Church in America and general issues like stewardship and church growth.

Some courses touched upon all four arenas of ministry. We believe it is important for Christians to be good listeners, and that in this world, where everyone seems to be in a rush, a skilled listener can offer an important ministry to others. Therefore, from time to time, we have offered a course in effective listening. Gift identification is another important course offered periodically because many of us cannot identify or do not acknowledge the gifts we have been given, or we take our gifts for granted. A short course in showing us how to identify our gifts can be of great help in our ministries in daily life. Similarly, a course in CPR by the Red Cross can potentially save a human life.

In every series we present, we try to show the biblical and theological connections to the topic. The series "Christians and the Constitution" provides a good example. We chose this topic because many Christians, on the one hand, believe that we should censor more movies, television, and magazines that portray violence and the sexual exploitation of women, and on the other hand, want to maintain freedom of expression. Many Christians support the principle of separation of church and state and yet are unhappy with bans on prayer at public school events and with exclusion of Christian symbols from town hall or courthouse lawns.

For the series, we invited several judges, one of whom is a member of our congregation, to speak on the freedom of speech and church-state issues, and the publisher of our local newspaper (also one of our members) to speak on freedom of the press. In all these discussions we drew upon the Bible to show how individual freedom is also in tension with one's responsibility to the larger community. Protestant theology is strong in this area. Luther said, "A Christian is free and independent in every respect, a bond servant to none. A Christian is a dutiful servant in every respect, owing a duty to everyone."[8] It is so tempting to seek black or white answers to faith and life problems; in fact, we usually live in the gray areas where we must search out the most responsible action to take —sometimes the "least worst," as one of my friends puts it.

Because we have a large congregation, we frequently can find members qualified to be resource persons for our various programs. When a special expertise is required that we cannot fill, we do not hesitate to secure outside resources (for which we offer an honorarium of $50 per Sunday). More often than not, the outside speakers return the money to us because they are delighted that a church has called upon them to share their knowledge and experience. For our own members, no honorarium is offered.

Getting Organized

The intention to have four planning groups ran into logistical problems early in our work. How would we do the scheduling? Bringing the chairs of the groups together to schedule programs revealed several difficulties. First, while our space limitations dictated that only two programs, in addition to the foundational course, could be offered in the same month, often either more or fewer than two programs had been proposed for the same month by the planning groups working alone. This meant that some of the chairs had to go back to their committees and ask them to reschedule their resource people for some other month. Second, the need to reschedule sometimes meant an outside resource person was no longer available. We decided too much time was being spent planning and rescheduling.

Pastor Al encouraged us to make a dramatic change. He suggested an independent board of directors for the center, which would have overall responsibility for planning in the four arenas of ministry, and a volunteer director with an independent budget within the overall congregational budget. The board adoped its own mission statement, which reads:

> The Mission of Holy Spirit's Center for Faith and Life is to provide opportunities and events for the members of the congregation and others to deepen their Christian faith through education, support groups and real life experiences in connecting faith and daily life so that they can carry out their Christian ministries in the totality of their lives.

So we now have a board of twelve persons with a wide diversity of occupational backgrounds, who serve three-year terms on a rotating basis. I serve as the director, and each year we submit the names of three new board members for confirmation by our congregation council. In addition, a church council member, our director of member ministries, and Pastor Rick sit in on board meetings to provide liaison with the leadership of the church. All three help with our planning. We meet every other month, usually in my home. At times ad hoc committees are formed, based on occupational experience, to do detailed planning for a particular program. Copies of our minutes are forwarded to the church secretary for inclusion in the minutes of the congregation council.

Secretarial work is done by a secretary on the payroll of my company. Neither the pastor nor any of the staff try to dictate what we should present as programs, although naturally we welcome suggestions from all people. Our annual budget is modest.

One organizational issue with which we still struggle is Sunday morning scheduling. Because we are running out of space in our present sanctuary, we have gone to three services. We first tried to have worship at 8:30, 10:00, and 11:00, with Christian education, including the Center for Faith and Life, at 10:00. That turned out to be a disaster. Many families brought their children to Sunday School at 10:00 and attended worship service then rather than adult education. That plan worked against two of our congregational principles: families should worship together, and Christian education is for all. We now have worship at 8:00, 9:00, and 11:00, with 10:00 reserved for education. It works for everyone except our Sunday School teachers, who miss adult education. We try to deal with this problem by rotating the teachers as much as possible. In order to move from one hour to the next, we must maintain a tight discipline of no more than fifty minutes for worship or education. (Holy Communion is celebrated at every worship service.)

The Congregation's Response

Where once our adult education program drew ten to fifteen people, today our attendance is about ninety to one hundred people, divided between our two tracks, and not counting the foundational courses, which usually are limited to ten to twelve people due to space availability. It is still not great for a congregation our size, but it is far ahead of where we were five years ago.

Although the evaluations of the center are very positive, our board is dealing with several weaknesses. First, many of our people are weak in Bible knowledge. Our answer to this is to try to offer biblical connections in all our programs. We sometimes have a theologian come in to provide the introductory session on a series. We had a teaching theologian lead the first two sessions of a seven-week study of the church and human sexuality to explore what the Bible has to say on sexual matters. Similarly, another teaching theologian spent the first two sessions of a seven-week study of hate and violence in America showing how hate and violence is depicted in the Bible. We had a teaching theologian do two sessions of a five-week series on feminism and the Bible. Still, while having this type of course introduction is helpful for those with little Bible familiarity, some of the old timers think this is not "real Bible study."

A second criticism is a complimentary one. "I don't know how to choose between two good programs," people complain. It is a problem when two strong programs are scheduled against each other. We had requests to video tape programs but discovered that very few people picked up the tapes for home viewing.

At times we hear the comment, "What's the difference between your programs and the same topic offered at a Kiwanis meeting?" We reply that (a) we are bringing worldly issues into the church, (b) these topics are being discussed by members of our community of believers among whom the Holy Spirit dwells, and (c) we try to provide the biblical-daily life connection on these topics.

Other Programs

The Center for Faith and Life offers one-day seminars, usually on Saturdays, for topics that do not lend themselves to Sunday morning, fifty-minute sessions. These programs are primarily targeted at families under great stress. We have quite a few families in which husband and wife both work full time away from home and worry about whether or not they are being good parents. Some families are financially extended, having overcommitted on large homes, new cars, club memberships, expensive vacations, and private schools. They are very vulnerable should one of the partners lose his or her job. It is heartbreaking to see some of these families crack under stress and break up. Our Center for Faith and Life tries to present programs designed to help these stressed-out families before they crack. One such program, "Enriching My Relationships," led by a professional counselor and open to anyone in the community, attracted about thirty people, mostly married couples but also a few who were dating. Child care was provided. We included a light lunch and we charged a modest participant fee that covered most of our expenses.

Because many of our members are extremely busy and lead such stressful lives, we offered the equivalent of an all-day seminar on managing time. We knew that the families that most needed this seminar could not give a full day to it. So we offered the first session on a Saturday morning in January and the second on a Saturday morning in February. In the month between sessions, participants were encouraged to record how they used their time during a typical week. It was an eye-opener for many. This financially self-supporting event was also open to the community, included child care, and again attracted about thirty people.

The Faith and Life Forum

In October 1995, we inaugurated an annual Faith and Life Forum. The entire community was invited to hear a prominent person discuss how faith can connect with daily life. Our first speaker was Loren Mead, and his presentation was most appropriate because Mead believes strongly that the church of the twenty-first century will carry out its mission through the ministries of its members who daily cross the boundaries between church and world. About 150 persons attended from a broad range of churches in our community. These lectures will not be financially self-supporting, but we consider them a gift from our congregation to our community.

For many years our congregation participated in round-robin Wednesday night Lenten services with five other congregations in our community. While the program was helpful in building cooperation and trust among the local clergy, few of the people in our congregation participated. Frankly, most of the services were dull—not worth the effort to secure child care.

We needed to try something different. Pastor Al suggested that our congregation offer a simple soup meal on Wednesdays, have an educational period, and then a brief worship service. He turned to the Center for Faith and Life to come up with an educational program that was both relevant to the lives of our people, in keeping with the mood of Lent, and meaningful to our youth. After doing a bit of a market survey, we decided to focus on "spirituality," a term that is frequently used both in the church and in the world but that is little understood in either place.

We called upon two outside speakers, one male and one female, from the religion department of a local college, to make presentations on alternate Wednesday evenings. We titled the program "From Soup to Spirituality," and it was an instant success. Families ate together, child care was available for the little ones during the educational period, and then families worshipped together. If one measures success in terms of numbers, we had ten times more participation than in the years of community worship services. The next year we offered the same type of program, titled "Diet, Dinner, and Devotions," with a presenter well known for his work in personal and family devotions.

Promotion

We promote all the events of the Center for Faith and Life in our newsletter and in the Sunday worship bulletins. If a well-known person, such as our U.S. congressional representative or one of our common pleas judges, is scheduled to speak, we put announcements in the two local newspapers and extend an open invitation to the community to attend. For special events, we also put up posters liberally around the church building. We do not ask or rely on our pastors to do any promotion for us.

The Monday Connection

At 7:00 A.M. on the first Monday of each month, September to June, about twenty people, who have committed to meet for the ten-month cycle, gather at the Superior Restaurant in Emmaus for a Dutch-treat breakfast. The event, called the Monday Connection, is both an equipping and a supporting event.

The waitress quickly takes orders around the large U-shaped table. After a few minutes of socializing, one of the members offers a prayer. Another member then passes out copies of a real-life case study of a problem or decision he or she is facing at the time. The case study usually is work-related but can involve family or community issues. As the waitress serves food, the Monday Connection participants read the case study.

Then the discussion begins. Initially, there are questions to gather additional information because seldom can a case be fully presented on one sheet of paper. Then the questions begin to change to "what ifs." These questions help the case study presenter to explore options. "What if you did _____?" or "Have you ever thought about _____?" Group members begin to debate the options among themselves. The presenter is never put on the defensive. Rather, the group works together on the problem given to them.

Their task is to determine what would be the best Christian response. What would Jesus have me do? is the implied question at all times. We never tell the presenter what to do. He or she must make the ultimate decision. It is our belief that within the gathered community of the faithful, God is speaking to us.

The topics we discuss may involve the effects of downsizing in business, questionable ethical policies, interpersonal problems with coworkers or supervisors, balancing workplace demands with family needs, and many other issues. Sometimes the problems are of a confidential nature. If so, papers are collected following the discussion and we all agree to confidentiality. In ten years of meetings, no one has ever breached the confidentiality promise.

One of our pastors attends as a participant. We also look to the pastor to bring up any relevant biblical or theological connections. Our director of member ministries always attends, not as an expert problem solver but in order to get a better grasp of the types of problems being faced by members of the congregation. There are times when we agree to pray for the presenter during the next month. We frequently also ask for updates from previous presenters. This is a form of accountability.

We have an iron-clad agreement that we will finish by 8:00 A.M. so people can go to work. The September-to-June commitment makes it easy for people to drop out if the program is not meeting their needs.

Each August one of our volunteers puts a notice of a new cycle in our parish newsletter and also sends a note to previous participants asking if they wish to be kept on the mailing list. From these notices we usually get names of about thirty interested people. About ten days before the first of each month, Lee Brockman, another volunteer, sends out reminder postcards, asking each participant to advise us by phone whether or not he or she will attend. Lee calls those who fail to respond. We are convinced that the combination of a postcard notice with phone follow up is what gives us the good attendance we regularly have—at 7:00 A.M. on a Monday. Of the thirty people on our mailing list, we usually have about twenty who can make it on any given Monday. Others travel or have job conflicts.

The occupational range of participants is broad. We have several managers, a number of technical people, the publisher of our local newspaper, some homemakers, and one or two retired people. The gender mix is usually about fourteen men and six or seven women.

The Monday Connection acts as an equipping program because it helps people discover how they can connect their faith to some difficult problems. It also serves as a supportive program because it is a place where any of the participants can share a problem and be assured of receiving concern and support from Christian friends. It can be replicated by small, medium, or large congregations or clusters of churches.

Lenten Luncheons

A number of years ago, recognizing that about fifteen of our members worked in center city Allentown, we offered a series of six Wednesday noontime, Dutch-treat lunches during Lent at a private club where one of our people held a membership. The program was simple. There was a fixed luncheon awaiting us as we arrived. Prayer was offered, and following the lunch one of our members spoke about his or her job. We asked each of the six speakers to deal with the following: (1) what I do in my work, (2) the kinds of problems and decisions I face, and (3) how I see my faith relating to my work. Questions and discussion followed. We were on our way back to our jobs by 1:00 P.M.

The Lenten lunches were a very effective way for us to learn about each others' jobs and struggles. Particularly moving to me was the time Bill Westley spoke about his job as a labor negotiator for a major cement company. Typically, in new contract negotiations both management and the union begin by overstating their wishes. Management may want to change work rules and offer a 3 percent pay increase. The union will refuse to relax work rules and insist on an 8 percent pay raise. The management representative, in this case Bill Westley, has to fight for the best deal for his company. "Many labor negotiators are not truthful in dealing with the other side," he said. "As a Christian, I feel I must be truthful with everyone—and yet, I am under intense pressure by my management to get the best deal." He paused and added, "Sometimes it tears me up." Ever since that luncheon, I cannot help but think of Bill Westley's difficult ministry when I see him at worship in our church.

As the number of people working in center city Allentown dropped, we gave up the program. It is presently being continued by a cluster of center city churches.

Connections

Connections is an adult study program that we have used for many years. The course is a thirty-session program based on Luther's Large Catechism. Through a variety of learning experiences, including workplace visits, participants learn how their faith and their daily lives are connected. Leaders for the course are one of our pastors and our director of member ministries, both of whom have received leadership training. While it is difficult to find people who will commit to a thirty-session course presented on weekday nights, each time *Connections* is offered (usually annually) about ten to twelve people, the ideal number, do sign up. Participants emerge from the program with a better understanding of Luther's *Catechism* and how it relates to daily life, especially as they visit each other's places of work. They tend to continue meeting as a small support group after the series has concluded. It is, without question, the most intensive and rewarding program we have to help people claim their ministries in daily life.

Weekend Retreats

A weekend retreat provides a wonderful opportunity for education and community building. The ideal format for families with small children is to have a family retreat. It solves the problem of securing child care for a full weekend. We had a wonderful one a few years ago. From Friday evening through Sunday lunch, a group of families went off to a retreat location for renewal and recreation. Early Friday evening featured some family activities such as skits, story telling, and songs. After the kids were in bed, the adults did some sharing.

An assignment board was posted for different families to take turns at kitchen duty and clean-up. Before each meal, one family offered the thanksgiving, usually the one traditionally used in their home.

On Saturday morning after breakfast, we had a creative time. The children did art work while the adults tried soap sculpture or poetry. Following lunch on Saturday, there was outdoor recreation and hiking with all the kids. In late afternoon, a few of the families jointly planned for Sunday worship. After the evening meal, there were table games and a movie before the kids went to bed. Afterward the adults discussed a faith-related topic.

After breakfast on Sunday, we had more craft time for adults and children. An assignment was made to go outdoors and bring back something that speaks of God's presence. The Sunday morning worship, planned by a few of the families, was a high point. Prayers were shared. After lunch, we all departed for home.

Adult-only retreats offer much more time for study and discussion, but if such events are impossible to schedule due to the need to get care for children, a family retreat provides many benefits for all.

Resource Materials

Like most congregations, we have a library of books, audiocassettes, and videocassettes, and like most church libraries, it is seldom used. To help members take advantage of materials, what is needed is a person who will actively promote use of the available resources. Each newsletter should have some item mentioning a new book, audiocassette, or video-tape. In congregations where this is done, libraries are used. It is that simple. (See the appendix of this book for suggestions for resources that might be used to build a core library on Ministry in Daily Life.)

Education Outside the Congregation

When seeking to equip the people of God for ministry in daily life, it is important to be aware of educational opportunities outside the congregation and to encourage people to use them. It is unrealistic to think that all adult Christian education goes on only within the congregational programs.

Each January our local conference of churches offers the six-week Lay School of Theology in which a wide variety of courses are offered. Many of them are Bible studies or topics related to ministries within the

church. Few relate specifically to Ministry in Daily Life, but that's all
right. The Lay School of Theology meets the needs of many people who
hunger for more adult education but have few options in their own congregations. Similarly, more seminaries are offering summer lay schools
of theology.

The local colleges and universities, in their efforts to relate better to
their communities, frequently offer lectures that can be very helpful for
those who seek to do ministry in the political and social service arenas of
life. Congregational education leaders should be on the mailing lists of
the colleges and universities so they can promote appropriate events to
the members.

Summary

The how-tos of doing Ministry in Daily Life are too readily ignored by
clergy. There is an assumption that if someone truly wants to carry out
a ministry in his or her place of work, for example, the battle has been
won. To use a military simile, it is like assuming that if civilians sign up
for military service in a time of war, nothing more is needed. No weap-
ons. No training. Nothing. So the church spends all its energy training
the officer corps and the band, while the soldiers are kept in the barracks.
Some army.

When people learn about our equipping programs, they frequently
shake their heads and sigh, "Our church isn't as large as yours" and "Our
pastor is already overloaded." Hogwash. Virtually everything we are
doing can be done by much smaller congregations. And with the excep-
tion of *Connections*, everything is designed and executed by laypeople.

Our people who weekly cross the boundaries between church and
world need help learning how to relate faith and daily life and how to be
effective in their ministries. We are trying hard to provide them with
good learning experiences. Every congregation should do the same.

CHAPTER 5

Supporting the People

And we would urge you . . . to admonish the careless, encourage the faint-hearted, support the weak, and to be very patient with them all.
(1 Thessalonians 5:14 NEB)

Very early in my career as a steel salesman in Michigan, I was faced with a troubling ethical situation that I didn't know how to handle. I talked it over with my wife Judy, but I felt the need to hear from others. Because I knew that Christian principles were involved, I went to my pastor. He listened politely and then made a suggestion that really would have violated a federal law. I was shocked that he knew so little about federal antitrust laws, but in retrospect I realize I was expecting far too much from him. He simply had no knowledge of the world in which I worked daily. When I explained why his solution was not workable, he suggested I talk with some other business people in the congregation. But I didn't know who they were, and the pastor himself could name only a few, none of whom I knew.

At that time, I belonged to a very warm congregation where no one ever had any "problems." Every Sunday morning, as we greeted each other with "How are you doing?" the replies came back: "Great" or "Fine." Was I the only one in the congregation with a problem? I felt like it, and I felt very lonely.

So I ultimately talked to my boss, hoping he would understand the Christian dimensions of the problem as I saw it. Fortunately, he was a Christian (I never knew it until then), and he gave me very good advice. Help came from another Christian who had experience in my world.

Many years later, in a city far from home, I faced another troubling situation that also had faith dimensions. I called Judy from the distant airport and said I would be home by 7:30 P.M. and badly needed to discuss my problem with our Focus group. She said she would get on the phone right away. ("Focus," which stands for Families of Christians, Uniting and Supporting, is an ecumenical support group we have been in for twenty-five years.)

When I walked into the living room of our house at 7:30, there were fifteen Focus members sitting in a circle, waiting for me. I came close to crying when I saw all these dear friends who had dropped everything to meet with me. I told them about the situation, answered many of their questions and got a number of "what if" suggestions for action. The basic question was, What would Jesus have me do in the situation? The process helped greatly to clarify the situation in my mind. We closed the evening in a joint prayer, during which I was overwhelmed with the sense of concern, love, and support for me.

The Need for Support

What was the difference between the two situations? I had a support group for the second one, but I felt virtually alone for the first. A congregation may affirm my Ministry in Daily Life, it may equip me to carry out my ministry effectively, but unless I feel the support of brothers and sisters in the faith, I am like a lonely ship feeling my way through a fog bank. The element of support is so critical, in fact, that when things were almost dangerously dull in our congregational life in one of the places we lived, our small group was the only thing that nurtured our spiritual needs.

Judy and I have been members of Christian support groups in each of the five congregations in which we held membership in the past thirty years. The close relationships we have developed have been extremely important in our growth in the faith. Our Face to Face group at St. Luke Lutheran Church in Devon, Pennsylvania, was such an important part of the lives of many of us thirty years ago that eight of us still meet once a year for a four-day weekend retreat at one of our homes, even though we are now widely scattered. We call ourselves the "Devon Eight."

In a generic sense, a support group consists of people with a shared mission who gather for the sole purpose of supporting each other in the area of their commonality. Alcoholics Anonymous gathers for the sole purpose of helping those who attend avoid alcohol. My wife, Judy, had polio when she was eighteen and recently has been feeling the debilitating effects of post-polio syndrome. She and similarly affected persons regularly meet in a polio survivors group in which they give each other emotional support as their motor problems increase. Parents Without Partners exists to give mothers and fathers who are raising a family without the help of a spouse the kinds of support needed to carry on. Similarly, Christians need support groups as they try to connect faith and daily life.

The committees that meet regularly to conduct the business of the congregation are seldom support groups. They meet for the specific purpose of caring for the property, planning Christian education, doing social ministry, rehearsing as a choir, and similar tasks. Their objective is to help meet the needs of the congregation. A true support group's objective is to meet the needs of its members for spiritual growth, intimacy, friendship, and caring.

Developing a Support Group

There were no formal support groups at Holy Spirit Church when we joined. Those who were charter members of the church were very close to each other and immediately responded with food, visits, and prayers when one of them became ill. They tended to have especially close social relationships with two or three other families, but nothing was structured. It was an informal support group—and it was closed. The charter members did not consider that new members needed support also, that church membership involved more than simply attending one hour of worship each week.

By the time we joined Holy Spirit, the congregation had grown close to four hundred and there was no way the supportive relationships of the charter members could be expanded to include us all. As a congregation we were at that point where, when we chatted before or after worship services, everything was "great." No one had any problems. Except by now I knew that was not so.

So Judy and I invited twelve other people to help us start a koinonia group. We explained that "koinonia" is the Greek word for "community"

or "fellowship." Among the fourteen of us, there were six couples, one
widow, and one single mother. Our ages ranged from over sixty to under
twenty-five. The purpose we established was to grow together in our
faith and to be supportive of each other in times of need.

We met the third Sunday evening of each month in one of our homes.
We agreed to start promptly at 7:30 P.M. and to conclude promptly at 9:30.
The host family would provide coffee and "no more than one thing to
eat." A piece of pie or cake was common.

The host family provided a short devotional reading and prayer.
Then we went around the circle to check in with each other. We reported
on things that had happened since last we met. As we grew to know and
trust each other, we began to share some rather deep concerns: a health
problem, worry over a child, a job concern. Once we heard fully from
everyone, we turned to our joint book study. The books were always of
a religious nature and provided much good discussion as we grew in our
faith. However, book study was secondary to "checking in." It was the
thing we turned to if none of us had a deep need to talk. At times, we
spent the entire evening in supportive conversation for one of us in need.

Our earliest call for support was when the single mother's three-year
old son was killed by an auto in front of their home. It was a deep trage-
dy, and all of us tried to reach out in many ways. Judy and I were in
Pam's home within hours. We all brought food for their meals. And we
sat as a group for the funeral. It was a highly emotional experience for us
all.

"Shepherd" Programs

When Pastor Tom arrived two years after we joined Holy Spirit, he immediately saw the need for more small support groups. He bought into a
"shepherding" plan, promoted by some national staff person who, in my
opinion, did not understand how support groups work. A large map was
produced, and the parish was divided into zones with approximately ten
member families in each zone. From each zone a "shepherd" was selected (sometimes with much arm twisting by the pastor) who would be
responsible for the other families in the zone. The idea was that each
zone would develop into a koinonia group so that if one family had a
need, the others would help.

It was also expected that church attendance would improve, thanks to the members of the group—or at least as a result of visits by the shepherd. A nice theory on paper, but it didn't work.

For one thing, when some families, especially those who were little more than nominal members, were told they had been assigned to a certain shepherd group, they politely (usually) said "No thanks." Second, the groups had no affinity other than the location of their homes. If some members had developed an affinity for one or two other families at the church, they were probably cut off from being in the same koinonia group with them because of where they lived. Finally, the shepherds had inadequate training and, in many instances, very little heart for the job. It was a total disaster and set back small group formation a good three years.

The shepherd program violates the basic purpose of a support group. As indicated earlier, a support group's purpose is to meet the needs of the members; the shepherd program is really designed to meet the needs of the institutional structure.

Varieties of Support Groups

Our Koinonia group is still together after twenty years. Only four of the original fourteen remain in the group. Five have moved away and five dropped out over the years. Other members have come and gone, but we now have a core group of twelve who attend all meetings, plus eight others who attend about half of our monthly gatherings. When all twenty are present, our group is much too big for a small living room, but due to members' work and travel schedules, we are seldom all together. In addition to our monthly meetings, we sometimes have picnics and regularly attend the Christmas carol service at Muhlenberg College.

Two other Koinonia groups of younger couples have been together for about eight years. One group jointly purchased a vacation home in North Carolina for time sharing and group retreats. Over the years, other support groups have developed. Because they tend to develop informally, we really don't know how many exist, but here is a sampling of some of them.

A support group of women who work at home as mothers, homemakers, or professionals calls themselves the "M and Ms" (for Mary and

Martha). They meet once a month for breakfast in the home of one of
the members. Their program format is similar to the koinonia groups: a
devotional period first, sharing of experiences second, book study next,
and prayer in closing. About ten to twelve are present at each session.

A similar group for women who work outside the home also meets
monthly in one of the members' homes. They call themselves the "3Ds"
(for dessert, devotions, and discussion). About eight to ten people regularly participate. As the name implies, they have dessert, followed by a
devotional moment led by the host. Discussion can center on individual
needs or a book study.

The COOL group (Coalition of Older Lutherans) is a rather large
group that meets once a month for lunch at the church building. Many
are charter members of the congregation. Most of them are in their 80s.
They are not into discussion but prefer to have someone come in with a
program. I list them as a support group, however, because they do look
out for each other. If one is sick or needs help of some kind, the rest
spring into action.

As *Connections* groups, explained in the previous chapter, complete
their studies, many continue to meet regularly and are developing into
support groups. The format varies. Some follow the pattern of Koinonia
groups; others are primarily social. A small prayer group meets weekly at
the church. While their primary mission is prayer, they too have a period
of sharing. A small group of men who are interested in spirituality meet
weekly with Pastor Rick in his office. They share daily experiences and
work on developing their own spirituality.

In times of high local unemployment, we activate a weekly support
group for those who are out of work. The group usually meets for a full
morning on Wednesdays at the church building. We secure professionals
to help with writing resumes, developing networks, and going for interviews. We also invite one or more of our members who recently went
through unemployment and job search to share his or her feelings. In the
years that we have activated this support group, there have been no more
than a half-dozen jobs found directly through the support group. But as
veterans reflect on the importance of the group, they invariably mention
that it provided a structured thing to do each week, and because of the
interaction with others who were out of work, they felt they were not
alone. "I discovered," says one veteran, "that my emotions weren't so
unusual after all, and that was very consoling."

Recent Retirees

A group of recent retirees—which includes those about to retire, those going through the retirement process, and those who have retired in the past three years—has formed. A number of the members have retired early, primarily due to corporate downsizing. These people are going through the shock of an unexpected retirement and are not at all ready to slow down. Twenty-six people are in the group. The group meets once a month at our church for a continental breakfast and an exchange of ideas and information. They have created seven interest subgroups that meet at various times and places. The interest groups include art, computers, small business, technology, sharing, intellectual stimulation, and finances. People have selected their own interest groups. Some are in only one; some are in as many as five. It should be no surprise that the largest interest subgroup is computers.

The Monday Connection

In the previous chapter, we described in detail how the Monday Connection operates. It serves both equipping and supporting functions. It equips members of the group to process daily problems in such a way that Christian perspectives can inform the ultimate decision. It is supportive because it provides participants with a group of Christian friends with whom they can share problems and from whom they receive caring support.

No "Little Churches"

In the early stages of the small group movement some clergy were concerned that the small groups would develop into little churches that would draw people away from full involvement in the larger congregation. It has not happened. All the members of Holy Spirit Church's varied small groups are faithful in Sunday worship and are supportive of the needs of the congregation. They are choir members, committee and council members, teachers, and volunteers.

I believe small groups enhance congregational life rather than detract from it. They provide the intimate, supportive atmosphere that people need and cannot get from a group of several hundred people who worship together each Sunday. Small groups are only a threat to the old-style pastor who must be in control of everything in the congregation.

Discernment Groups

Another type of support group that has been very helpful is a discernment group. A discernment group has as its sole purpose helping people determine what their particular Christian calling might be at the present time. It is by nature a small and very intimate group of friends. It should number no less than six nor more than ten.

We were introduced to this intimate support group by Suzanne Farnham, coauthor of the book *Listening Hearts: Discerning Call in Community*.[9] After reading about the process, six of us agreed to give the discernment process a try. Each of us was facing the opportunity to make a change in our lives Some were minor changes, some major. Each person was asking the question, What would Jesus have me do at this point in my life? That question has the best chance of being answered in the company of a few loving Christian friends who care greatly about us. "Where two or three are gathered in my name, I am there among them" (Matt. 18:20).

The process was that each person, in turn, would write up his or her current life situation, describe the opportunity facing him or her, and list his or her own reasons for and against making the change. Each person's paper would then be sent to the other five at least a week prior to our coming together. The other five were asked to review the paper and pray daily for wisdom that might be of assistance.

We agreed to gather in one of our homes in connection with a meal. We felt that a shared meal would be a good preface for trying to discern the ministry of one of our sisters or brothers. When it was my turn, I wrote a paper in which I said that for most of my adult life I had intentionally kept one foot firmly in the world of business and the other firmly in the institutional church. I felt that balance had always given me credibility in my writing and public speaking. Soon, I pointed out, I would conclude almost twenty-five straight years of serving on national boards and church councils of the Evangelical Lutheran Church in America and

a predecessor church. How would I maintain that one foot in the organized church, apart from participating in congregational life, which I had
always done? I saw four options: First, I could work within my local
synod on Ministry in Daily Life. Second, I could submit my name for
membership on another national board of the ELCA. Third, I could put
energy into helping to start an ecumenical coalition of people working to
advance Ministry in Daily Life. Finally, I could spend more time doing
conferences, seminars, and retreats on Ministry in Daily Life.

   As we shared the meal on "my day" for discernment, there were
many questions about the four options. They wanted more information,
particulary about my sense of my enthusiasm for each option. I was affirmed in my strong vision of Ministry in Daily Life and in my talent for
being creative and starting new things. The more we talked, the more
obvious it became that I saw a challenge in helping to develop a coalition
for Ministry in Daily Life. It became a choice between continuing to do
things in areas where I had experience and a high comfort level, and
launching out into a new and interesting venture. We talked and prayed
and, as we did, I felt a strong sense of call to a new ministry—The Coalition for Ministry in Daily Life.

   Each month, one of us had his or her "day," and after six months we
discontinued the discernment process, except for one thing. The six of us
had bonded so closely in our efforts to help each other that we still get
together for dinner from time to time to see how things are going. I feel
strongly that through the prayers and discussions with close friends, God
has been calling me to a new venture. Furthermore, I have a special need
to let my five colleagues know how that new venture is going.

Support Groups in the Workplace

My first effort to develop a Christian support group at my workplace was
a failure. I contacted a group of ten Bethlehem Steel employees whom I
knew from my church activities belonged to other Lutheran churches in
town. I suggested that we have lunch together. At our first gathering I
pointed out that we all had at least two things in common: we were active members of Lutheran congregations in the area and we worked for
the same employer. In what ways did these two facts connect, I asked? I
had envisioned that we would talk about how our faith related to the

problems and decisions we faced at Bethlehem Steel. It never turned out that way. Each time we met the conversation quickly turned to comparing notes on what was going on in each other's churches, how they conducted adult education, how they ran their stewardship campaigns, who did the visiting of prospective members. On and on it went until it seemed all the comparisons had been exhausted. Now, I thought, we'll get down to the *real* stuff, the business of faith and daily life. Wrong again! They decided to stop meeting because "there wasn't much to talk about anymore." The connection between our church life and our business life was never made.

A second try was made with Pastor Tom Reinsel. This time we worked only with members of our own congregation who worked at Bethlehem Steel. I invited about ten of our own members to have lunch with the pastor in a small room outside the cafeteria at our research center. Six showed up. We went through the food line, had our lunch, and settled in for a discussion with Pastor Tom. I started out by telling of a real life problem I was facing with an employee who, due to the misjudgment of former management, was in a job unsuited to his talents. He was regularly underperforming in his work. What should be done with him?

A good discussion ensued. Was it fair to terminate or even demote him, given that it was management that made a mistake? After all, we don't scrap equipment that does not perform as expected. We try to work with it. Shouldn't we treat people at least as well as equipment? No sir, responded some. If he doesn't perform, in spite of your efforts to coach him and help him, you must get rid of him. Then I asked if God scraps us when we underperform. Doesn't God accept us in spite of our failures?

This provided an opening for Pastor Tom to talk about the grace of God and also the law of God. Yes, God is forgiving, but God also calls us to tend God's creation. As managers, we do not act responsibly if we do not work to uphold and extend God's creation. If every manager in every job in every part of the world accepted inferior performance from his or her workers, God's creation would suffer. The discussion was hard going for some of us, but we were truly injecting theology into the workplace.

The lunches continued for a few months, but dwindling participation told us that we had best conclude the lunches with the pastor. A few years ago, Pastor Al had similar lunches with members of our congregation who worked at Air Products. These, too, gradually faded.

I think there are two reasons for these failures. First, when most of God's people cross the boundary line from church to work, they give little conscious thought to God's presence. As pointed out in the first chapter to this book, it is off limits. The second reason is more pragmatic. To really deal with issues of faith in the workplace requires an honest sharing of how things are, like my case of the employee who was underachieving. It can be dangerous to open up about workplace issues when one is in the workplace. Who knows what may get passed along until it gets into the wrong hands? It is much safer to talk about such things in the greater security of a koinonia group or a Monday Connection breakfast.

At the same time as I was trying to develop support groups at Bethlehem Steel, I was aware that at least one Bible study group met once a week and that there was also a prayer group. My questioning of those involved revealed that the groups stuck strictly to Bible study and prayer for the healing of associates. No effort was made to connect faith to the experiences of life in that workplace.

Based on my experiences and observations of a number of groups, I wonder whether we expect occupational support groups to function freely at the place of work. Or should we see the neutral ground of the restaurant or the living room as the place where workers share the experiences of the workplace and seek to make faith connections with them?

Accountability

The question arises as each of us goes about our ministry in daily life, To whom are we accountable? To God? Yes, of course. But God doesn't give us direct verbal feedback from on high. In our work we are accountable to our employer. In fact, many of us receive annual performance reviews in which we get feedback on how well we are doing. In my management consulting work, I am accountable to my clients. In our congregations the pastor and staff persons are accountable to the governing board for the quality of their work. They get helpful feedback from the board.

The wonderful feature of a support group is that it can and should give us feedback about our daily life ministries. We are accountable to our support group, not in the sense that we are to an employer but in the sense that we answer to people who have invested their time, energy, and caring in our situations. Because we know each other intimately and care for each other, members are concerned about how the others are doing in daily life ministry.

Those of us who participated in the discernment group share a type of accountability. When I discuss a pressing work problem or a worrisome family problem with my Koinonia group, at the next meeting and frequently in between sessions they will ask me how I'm doing. More than once I have received a phone call from a member of my Koinonia group asking how I am doing with a particular situation.

It is interesting to observe that even at our Monday Connection breakfasts, when a person shares his or her workplace problem with the group and in return gets some suggestions from the group, there are almost always follow-up inquiries a month later. Questions such as "How did you do?" or "Whatever happened to _____?" invariably are directed to the previous month's presenter. Support groups provide the best means for feedback and accountability in our ministries in daily life. And we might even say that one of the reasons we *need* support groups is so that we have someone to whom we are expected to hold ourselves accountable.

CHAPTER 6

The Pastor's Role

The gifts he gave were that some would be . . . pastors and teachers to equip the saints for the work of ministry. (Ephesians 4:11, 12)

Can a congregation have an active program for Ministry in Daily Life if the pastor is dead set against it? You know the answer. It's no. Can *anything* happen that affirms, equips, and supports God's people for ministry in such a congregation? Actually, yes. There is nothing to stop laypeople from having small groups that meet in homes or for breakfasts in restaurants. Many materials are now available that will help such groups get started. The pastor may look with disfavor on such lay-initiated groups but, hey, it's a free country, isn't it?

It has been my experience that the reaction of clergy to the principle of Ministry in Daily Life is like a typical bell curve. At the one extreme of the bell curve are those few pastors who are adamantly opposed to the notion that everyone has a ministry. They see Christian ministry as a zero sum game in which any elevation of the laity's ministry lowers the ministry of the ordained. At the other end are pastors who are very excited about lay ministry and are constantly searching for ways to make it work in their church. These pastors see the ministry of the laity as a multiplier of the ministry of the clergy.

In the middle of the bell curve are the preponderance of clergy, who truly believe in the concept of the ministry of all God's people but who are so tied to the traditional ways of doing ministry and so inculcated by what they have been taught in seminary that they can't seem to break free to really support Ministry in Daily Life in their congregations.

These pastors truly believe that if they have lay people assist in the worship service, if they have an annual "Laity Sunday," and if they occasionally preach on the importance of laypeople connecting their faith with their daily lives, people will be motivated and equipped to carry out daily life ministries. Pastors who believe this are dead wrong.

Holy Spirit Church's Pastors

When Judy and I joined the Lutheran Church of the Holy Spirit in 1974, Pastor Walter Kuntzleman, the first pastor the congregation ever had, was nearing retirement. He was open to suggestions about how to help people make their faith-life connections, and when we suggested forming a koinonia group, he and his wife were eager to join.

Tom Reinsel came in 1976 after Pastor Kuntzleman retired. He and I began to have breakfasts together, and I shared with him my frustrations with inward-looking congregations and my visions for Ministry in Daily Life. Tom resonated with talk about Ministry in Daily Life for two reasons. First, his past two parish experiences were in rural congregations. For him, visiting members frequently meant chatting in the barn or out in an open field as the farmer worked. He says that the people appreciated that he accepted them just as they were. The second factor was that Tom's wife, Amy, became a director of volunteers for a local agency. She saw volunteerism as ministry. "Before long," Tom says, "I began to think that volunteerism outside the church was an OK ministry."

Tom began his workplace visits with me at Bethlehem Steel and followed up with many more parishioners, as described in chapter 3. He began group luncheon meetings at places where several of our members worked for the same employer. He even was given his own security badge by one of the major companies in our area. During Tom's time with us, we started the "Ministry in _____" programs, the Monday Connection breakfasts, and the downtown Lenten luncheons. At each new suggestion, Tom was immediately supportive. Increasingly his sermons were laced with daily life experiences and were very affirming of Ministry in Daily Life.

Tom reflects, "When I made calls on a member whose worship attendance was poor, I always started the conversation with a question about how things were going in their daily lives. As the problems surfaced, I would say, 'You are not being fueled for these problems. You need to be with us in worship in order to deal with the daily problems you face.'"

I once asked Tom what his advice would be to a pastor who really wanted to start supporting Ministry in Daily Life in his or her congregation. "That's easy," he replied. "The first thing to do is to begin visiting people where they work. You don't necessarily want to start with high profile members. All people love to tell you what they do. Show them you are truly interested in them."

"And then?" I asked.

"Gather your Ministry in Daily Life resources together and see what makes the most sense to do next," he replied.

"What resources?"

"Oh, during your visits with members, you may spot one or two members who are ready to provide leadership for Ministry in Daily Life in the congregation. Or you may use programmatic resources produced by your own denomination or other organizations. Maybe your local synod or diocese can provide help. It's out there. You just need to search a bit."

After serving Holy Spirit Church for about eleven years, Tom accepted a call to another congregation. Like most congregations that lose a beloved pastor, we thought we could never replace him. When the congregation council drew up the job description for the new pastor, the description included a strong emphasis on Ministry in Daily Life. During the interviews with candidates, the call committee asked a number of questions about Ministry in Daily Life. We knew what we wanted, but did the candidates know what we were looking for? Among those who did was Pastor C. Alton Roberts. His many talents and his past experience were what we needed. He accepted our call and became the third senior pastor of Holy Spirit.

An Interview with Pastor Al Roberts

Bill: Al, to what extent did you incorporate Ministry in Daily Life into your work before coming to Holy Spirit Church?

Al: From the very beginning of my ministry I sensed that there was a big gap between what I perceived to be a fairly clearly defined role for me as a pastor in the congregation and a less clearly defined role for the members, especially in what they did Monday through Friday.

Early in my ministry I invited the laity to be more involved in worship, and that was the extent of my understanding of the ministry of the laity. I believed it wasn't just the prerogative of the pastor to do everything in the liturgy, and so even before it became popular in other congregations, I had laity distributing bread, being involved with reading the lessons and all the things we do today that we seem to take for granted. I sensed that people were not making connections between their faith and daily life because I never heard them talk about their faith in terms of their business or teaching. I guess I was aware that there was a problem, but it was very vague and not well focused for me.

Bill: So does that mean that when you were interviewed for your position at Holy Spirit, it became more focused? What was your reaction to the job description at Holy Spirit?

Al: I had heard about Holy Spirit and it's work with Ministry in Daily Life. I felt that, if called to Holy Spirit, it would be a great learning opportunity. I was quite aware of the theology of the priesthood of all believers but knew that much work had to be done on the practice of it. I saw that the people of Holy Spirit were quite open to working on the implementation of that theology. That was exciting.

Bill: In what ways has your understanding of Ministry in Daily Life changed since coming to Holy Spirit?

Al: It has changed in many ways. I have grown in my understanding of the priesthood of all believers, which has really never caught on because of the structure of the church. I've learned more about everyone being called by God in baptism for ministry. I've also learned how difficult it still is for people to believe this and that it will be for some time to come. I believe it is not possible for clergy to teach plumbers or bankers how to do their ministry in daily life. We must work at it together.

On the one hand, I can see the real possibility of all the people of God doing ministry in the roles and places where God has placed them. On the other hand, I have discovered that the problem is much worse than I first thought. I see a lot of challenge and a great deal of effort is going to be needed in the future to really make this work. For me, I think the biggest thing I've learned, if I were to sum it up, would be that Ministry in Daily Life is not simply another emphasis in the church; it *is* the church. There is no other church. I think that is hard for a lot of other clergy to buy. I think to really be engaged in Ministry in Daily Life is nothing short of fully living your life in the presence of God, which is a very deeply spiritual matter. So I can look at Ministry in Daily Life and say it is something that is finally being lifted up and needs to be focused on because it has been ignored too long. When you do that you see all of the other aspects of Christian faith very clearly—spirituality, stewardship, worship, outreach—you go right down the list and Ministry in Daily Life is the core of it.

Bill: In what ways do you feel you have shaped the congregation's understanding of ministry in daily life? I think we have grown since you have come here.

Al: I guess I see myself as the pastor of the congregation, the one who can articulate the vision to people in sermons, in the way I speak at committee meetings, in the way I try to help restructure the way our congregation operates by having the pastor and the council not be controlling but empowering. I think once I caught the vision and focused on the issues, I was able to reshape my ministry and the way I am with people. I always ask the question, How does this thwart or how does this advance members' understanding of their call in baptism? I think that has been my role.

Bill: What do you see as an obstacle to promoting Ministry in Daily Life in a congregation, not just meaning ours but take any congregation, what are the obstacles you see?

Al: I think that one of the problems the Christian church faces is that it doesn't really see that there is a serious problem, that this is not something that is simply a matter of nomenclature, of naming things. It goes a lot deeper than that. And I think the congregations don't realize how serious the problem is. Therefore, they might think, "Oh, we do this pretty well. We tell everybody they are Christians all day, twenty-four hours a day. What else do they need to know?" Well, you need to know a lot more than that. How *are* you a Christian twenty-four hours a day? For a lot of folks, trying to find God at the work place in certain situations is tough sledding. You know, things are not always clear; they're very ambiguous. And where *is* God in this mess I'm in, or in this decision to fire this person, or in this family difficulty of mine? So I think that one of the problems is admitting that there *is* a problem. The church has kind of glossed over its inadequacy.

Second, and this is a real tough one, how do you structure a congregation so that all of its energy, and all of its advertising, and all of its communicating isn't simply about what's happening in house? And that is really a tough issue. I don't think the paradigm of church as we have it now, where the pastor does all the ministry for the congregation, is really the best paradigm. The pastor takes care of the sick, the pastor visits those in the hospital, the pastor counsels those who have spiritual and psychological problems, the pastor is involved in the community, the pastor works for low income housing for downtown Allentown, and on and on. So Ministry in Daily Life will be the liberation of the clergy, and I don't think they always understand that.

Bill: Are new clergy being prepared for this? Is the seminary making any kind of shift that prepares clergy for this different view of the role of the laity?

Al: From what I have seen of graduates coming out of the seminary, I would say no. Seminaries prepare people to do ministry in the paradigm that the seminaries themselves have been created out of. That's understandable. When I spoke to the dean of one of our seminaries about six months ago and expressed to him my concerns about this whole issue of the ministry in daily life and what is the seminary doing, he said, "Well, we're going to have someone come in and give a lecture and have a course." I said, "That's really not going to do the job. I'm talking about when will the seminary begin to examine how it prepares pastors so that they have some clue as to their role in helping plumbers minister to other plumbers, carpenters minister to other carpenters, and nurses minister to other nurses, and to developing a cadre, a family of faith, that is a launching pad for the real ministry of the church?" "Well, we're not quite that far along yet," he said.

Bill: What advice would you give to a pastor who wants to implement Ministry in Daily Life into a congregation with no past history of it? Where does he or she start?

Al: I would say you have to start with prayer. I've become more and more aware of prayer as the source of inspiration—God going with you —meaning I've never arrived anyplace where God hasn't been there first. Then I would say, the pastor ought to seek out, listen carefully, interview people, visit and talk with folks, and find, I'm sure, a few people who already have some sense of Ministry in Daily Life and already have some commitment to helping others see their Ministry in Daily Life. And then, working with these people, come up with a plan. I really think you need to have a plan of vision, of what this congregation could be like. And then begin to implement the plan. I don't think a pastor can go off into his office and come up with this plan. I think he or she has to be actively involved in partnership with laity. You've got to do it with the people that God has sent to you, to be your mentors in this. I know how to do Word and Sacrament. I don't know how to do Ministry in Daily Life as an accountant. And if I haven't got a clue into this one, I've got to talk to an accountant. And not all accountants know how to do that. See, that's the problem. But there will be some who do.

Bill: OK, so you're saying that when the pastor meets with some lay persons who have a good sense of Ministry in Daily Life, they can work together toward some kind of plan for the congregation.

Al: Yes, and it could be that the plan would be to start organizing small groups around the discussion of Ministry in Daily Life. I really don't think most lay people are averse to that. I think it's a rather attractive thought. People like to talk about what their work is like. I think that would work and as the movement builds in the congregation, start asking council people to be involved in this discussion. Think about this. What can I do in sermons? What can we do in programs? What can we do in adult ed? What can we do with children in Sunday school?

Bill: In our congregation we have our pastoral leadership and lay leadership that's working in Ministry in Daily Life. Do you feel confident that Ministry in Daily Life is so woven into the fabric of our congregation that it will continue regardless of loss of present leadership?

Al: I would say no. I've just been around too long, and I have been in two parishes where the pastor who followed me did things completely opposite, and it wasn't too long before the people were marching to a different drum.

Bill: So we get back to the pastor thing again.

Al: Yes.

Bill: Are you saying that even if the congregation has a very strong sense of Ministry in Daily Life, it's still possible for a pastor to come in and, in a sense, erase it all?

Al: Sad to say, I think yes. I've seen it. But I don't think it's guaranteed. I think if a new pastor came to Holy Spirit and was opposed to Ministry in Daily Life, there would be a heck of a battle. And either the pastor would lose that battle and move on, or more likely the people who latch on to Ministry in Daily Life would move on. Unfortunately, there will always be enough people rallying to the side of a pastor that it makes removal very difficult.

Bill: That's a kind of dismal note on which to end our interview. If I hear you, what you are saying is that in the end all the work we have done could all be for nothing if the new pastor wishes it to be so.

Al: Yes, it may sound dismal, but I think there is also a great warning here. The congregation in our system has a major role to play in choosing its leadership. So I think that a high priority, *the* highest priority is to question the candidates seriously on how they feel about Ministry in Daily Life. Do they see any conflict in their understanding of pastoral leadership and affirming the ministry of all the people of God? How does that affect worship, and how does that affect education, and so on? So I don't think it's dismal. I think it's realistic. And if Ministry in Daily Life ultimately grows to the point where it will be difficult for a pastor to find any parish that doesn't require this understanding, then you've changed the paradigm. But, for now, you must be cautious. The call committee has a *very* important role to play.

Bill: So with a job description that focuses on Ministry in Daily Life and a call committee that is strongly in support of it, a congregation can survive a loss of leadership?

Al: Absolutely, but those two things must be present.

Bill: Thanks, Al, for this brief chat. I'm sure it will be of help to pastors and congregational leaders.

Elton Trueblood said it well:

> The ministry is for all who are called to share in Christ's life, but the pastorate is for those who possess the peculiar gift of being able to help other men and women to practice any ministry to which they have been called.[10]

Meanwhile, Back at the Seminary

From time to time I have the opportunity to chat with seminary presidents and deans. In the course of the conversation, I ask, What is the measure of success of your seminary? The answers can be summed up as follows: "We are successful if we turn out well-motivated, well-equipped, and well-educated church leaders."

It seems to me that such was the measure of seminary success in the so-called Christendom age of the church. This was when church leaders enjoyed high public esteem, when the laity were passive members to whom the clergy ministered, and when the mission field was in far-off lands. However, it is the premise of this book that the Christendom age has almost disappeared. In this multicultural, individualistic society, church leaders, like leaders of most of our institutions, do not enjoy great public esteem and the mission field is right outside the walls of our church buildings. The measure of success of seminaries today should be, "We are successful if we are ultimately responsible for a well-motivated, well-equipped, and well-educated church."

I dislike using a military simile for the church, but we do not judge the success of our military academies on the quality of the officers they turn out. The ultimate success of the military academy is measured by whether the army or navy can win a war in the field. And if we cannot win wars, then changes have to be made back at the military academies. Similarly, the success of the seminary should be judged by the degree to which the church (which is 99 percent laity) is bringing the Gospel of Jesus Christ to the world, both in word and deed. That's what Pastor Roberts meant when he told the dean of a seminary that having a lecture and one course on the ministry of the laity "is not going to do the job."

Seven Suggestions for Pastors

If we focus on the church, primarily through its laity, ministering to the world, what should a parish pastor be doing? Here are my seven suggestions:

1. Be a believer. Truly believe that the church is to minister in the world and that the laity have been called to do it. If you can't believe in this, then stop reading here.

2. Listen. Ask your members to tell you what they do in their daily routines. Once they believe you are truly interested, they will tell you. People love to talk about their daily work. Listen to their stories and remember them.

3. Affirm, affirm, affirm. By the grace of God, your members are already in the mission field doing the things their God-given talents have best prepared them to do. Affirm that their work is important to God. Affirm that they have a ministry. And do it over and over again. They have been raised in a church that told them only *you* were the minister. So you need to preach again and again that their work matters to God.

4. Be patient. Remember what you are about is a radical change for people. It will take time for them to recognize their ministries. Don't be surprised or discouraged if they don't respond with eagerness. After all, being a passive pew sitter and not troubling one's mind about faith in daily life is a very comfortable way to practice religion. You are asking them to begin a religious life that is infinitely more difficult—and scarier.

5. Equip. Together with them find the ways they can best carry the Gospel into the world. Help them to make the connections between Sunday and the rest of the week. Help them to help each other.

6. Nourish. Make sure the word you preach, the sacraments they receive, and the worship they experience each Sunday will nourish them for the week to come.

7. Support. Help them to create their own support groups. You don't have to do it. Just give them the vision and resources.

Before you gasp about all the things you have to do, remember this is a new model and that ministry in the church is one of four arenas of ministry for the laity. Laity are to be active, not passive, in the internal workings of their local church. It is much too early to see how congregations would be structured, but Davida Crabtree's experience at

Colchester Federated Church gives one possible model. Ideally, all the administrative, financial, committee, and programmatic work of the local church should be handled by laypeople. There is no reason why laypeople should not make hospital visits and prospective member calls once everyone understands the universal priesthood of the baptized. The pastor would then be freed up to be the teacher, preacher, and supporter of ministry in the world. It would be similar to the situation in the early church, where seven helpers were selected to handle administrative work so that the twelve apostles would be freed up to give their "attention to prayer and the ministry of the word" (Acts 6:4 NIV). We are a long way from this condition, but in the transition period from where we are to where we will be, some of the many expectations currently placed on pastors can begin to change immediately.

CHAPTER 7

The Director of Member Ministries

Therefore, friends, select from among yourselves seven of good standing, full of the Spirit and of Wisdom, whom we may appoint to this task. (Acts 6:3)

In all but the smallest of congregations, there usually is a person whose responsibility it is to help with the recruitment of committee members, Sunday school teachers, ushers, and other volunteers for the work of the church. As Holy Spirit Church grew, the job of coordinating volunteers grew with it. The demands for volunteers became so heavy that we began burning out our coordinators. When that happened, the task fell back on the pastor, but we were not paying him to take care of coordination of volunteers.

It soon became obvious that we needed a full-time, paid person who would have complete responsibility for securing volunteers for all our congregational tasks. We also wanted someone who would help our members develop their ministries in daily life. We decided to place an ad in the local newspaper for a director of Lay Ministry. That's when Roberta Longsworth came to us.

"When I saw that ad for a director of lay ministry," Roberta reflects, "I knew exactly what they wanted. I had heard all about Christians in ministry in their daily lives in my own Presbyterian church, but I was not aware of any programs designed to support or affirm people in their ministries."

At the time, Roberta was director of the Volunteer Services Department at one of our community's large hospitals and was happy with what she was doing. "I knew I had an important ministry just where I was," she says. "But, when I saw that title for a church position, I thought 'That must be a *very* interesting congregation.'"

As it turned out, Roberta was the only one of five applicants who had the slightest idea of what the job was about. Most of the others thought a director of lay ministry was one who oversaw the Christian education program.

One of the attractions for Roberta was that it was a new job with only the sketchiest of job descriptions. She would be able to help develop the job description. One of the requirements was to help interpret "lay ministry" to our members. She was eager to give that a try, and we were happy to have her as a member of our staff.

First, she began addressing the issue of volunteerism in our congregation and began making some changes. Many churches and other organizations, when they go out to recruit helpers, make the mistake of selling the task in as minimal a way as possible. "It's only one short meeting a month" or "It won't take much of your time" are the typical appeals. Roberta's approach was different: She saw to it that every volunteer position had a written job description with specific expectations.

At first, our people laughed at the idea. "A job description for a *greeter*?" they chortled. But Roberta's philosophy was sound. "If you don't ask for much, you won't get much," she contends. "But give people written expectations and good training and you will almost always get high performance." Like Kathy Crane, a former coordinator of lay ministry at the First Presbyterian Church in Ithaca, New York, Roberta used the word "ministry" in these position descriptions: the "ministry of teaching," the "ministry of hospitality," the "ministry of committee service."

Roberta shared some of the Ministry in Daily Life teaching tasks with the pastor. She co-led the *Connections* program and helped with the "Ministry in _____" series. She completely revised the "time and talents" forms that we ask all members to fill out each year. Whereas the time and talents forms had always been exclusively related to tasks that needed to be done in the congregation, the new forms also dealt with ministries in the community. Interest items such as "drive Meals on Wheels," "work at food kitchen," "visit in prisons," and many more began to appear. Quite a few people checked off some of these interests with the result that we have become a place where many human service agencies seek volunteers.

As new members joined our church, Roberta visited each one of them in their place of work. She interviewed them to learn of their talents and affirm their ministry. People were suspicious about her intentions, feeling she wanted to recruit them for congregational tasks. Instead, she was interested in the prospects of their ministry in the church *and* in the world. More than once, after hearing what a new member was doing, Roberta would say, "Some day I may ask you to take over a responsibility in our congregation because you have many talents. But right now you are very busy with important ministries in which we want to affirm and support you." A number of new members have since reported that they couldn't believe someone from a church would talk like that.

Due to some health problems in her family, Roberta felt she needed to resign. But by then we had a detailed job description and a precise knowledge of the kind of person we needed to take over Roberta's spot. Pastor Roberts suggested we change the position title from "director of lay ministry" to "director of member ministries." It was another good step in our effort to stop using the "lay."

Then we faced a new problem. Roberta had so well defined the position for us that none of our candidates came close to meeting our needs on the first round of interviews. We advertised a second time, and among our next round of applicants was Pam Bonina. She had an in-teresting work background that included being a coordinator of volunteers for a local human service agency. In addition to her impressive credentials, she was willing to take a deep pay cut in order to come with us. This was a job she wanted, and together with her past work experience, she was the one we wanted.

I have asked Pam to conclude this chapter by expressing in her own words what has been exciting and appealing to her in the position of director of member ministries.

My Story—Looking Back

by Pam Bonina

It was a typical chilly, gray Pennsylvania morning in January. The snow on the ground outside seemed to make the inside all the more cozy and inviting. The Saturday paper lay open on the kitchen table, and for no particular reason, I started to glance through the classified employment section. At this time, I had no strong intentions of changing jobs. I was happy enough directing the local chapter of a national nonprofit organization. Our family had recently been through the tragic death of my husband's mother in a head-on automobile accident. His father, who became blind and disabled, was in our continued care. This event had made me stop and take a hard look at things: life, death, my faith and spirituality. I did not realize it then, but I was ready for a change.

The ad read: "The Lutheran Church of the Holy Spirit is seeking a person to fill the position of Director of Member Ministries." It went on to describe the position and state qualifications. The word "ministry" stymied me. I had no theological background; I was not a "clergy" person; and furthermore, I had been Lutheran for only one year. But I did have two years' experience managing volunteers, some teaching experience, excellent communication, organizational, and interpersonal skills." I decided to send a resume.

On March 7, 1994, I sat behind my desk at Holy Spirit Church for the first time. Part of me felt wonderful. Part of me felt scared. Somehow, I had faith that the Lord had brought me to this place, so I dug in. My biggest challenges seemed to be in learning the system, getting to know the 1,600-member congregation and learning more about a concept totally new to me: "Ministry in Daily Life." "The Holy Spirit Empowers Us for Ministry in Daily Life," the congregation's mission statement, was printed on our letterhead, job descriptions, church directory, even the coffee cup sitting on my desk. What did this mean?

Education was necessary. I decided to become a student of Ministry in Daily Life. I had read *Christianity and Real Life* (Bill Diehl, no longer in print) the week prior to coming to Holy Spirit. It had whetted my appetite, so I devoured more titles: *Faith Goes to Work* (Robert Banks), *The Monday Connection* (Bill Diehl), *Your Other Vocation* (Elton Trueblood, no longer in print), Evangelical Lutheran Church in America

materials on Ministry in Daily Life. To supplement my understanding
of Ministry in Daily Life and to understand where the church was headed
in the twenty-first century, I completed *The Once and Future Church*
(Loren Mead) and *The Empowering Church* (Davida Foy Crabtree). *How
to Mobilize Church Volunteers* (Marlene Wilson) seemed a good bridge
from nonprofit volunteer management to congregation empowerment.
My journey as director of member ministries had begun.

As I grew and have continued to grow, as I learned and have continued to learn, what have I noticed? What could I share with others? I
have become an impassioned student and advocate of Ministry in Daily
Life. How could I help others to embrace the belief? My faith and spirituality have been on the move.

One month after my beginnings at Holy Spirit, I was invited to a
Connections training event in New Jersey. The course focuses on new
ways of viewing Ministry in Daily Life connected to the Word, one's
daily life experiences, and one's faith. Roberta Longsworth had facili-
tated *Connections* when she was at Holy Spirit. Now it was my turn. As
I write, we are in our second year with a second group of members matri-
culating through *Connections*. I truly believe one of the greatest joys of
my ministry is to help others to see how God is with them seven days a
week and how they are ministering in their worlds. I must admit that I
had assumed that only clergy were called, and only clergy ministered to
the people. In fact, I came to realize I had been called and that my journey of ownership and belonging was just beginning. By virtue of my
baptism, I had been welcomed into the ministry of the whole people of
God. In some ways I regretted that it had taken me until midlife to realize this. No time to waste now.

The Job

My job description states that the director of member ministries "serves
as a key resource person for programs and activities which equip, support, and affirm the whole people of God for ministry in the church and
in the world." We are a large congregation at Holy Spirit. I inherited a
legacy of belief and buy-in to the concept of Ministry in Daily Life. But
I want to emphasize that what I do and how it is done can be applied to
volunteers in the small country church as easily as the larger, urban one.
It can be applied to churches of all denominations and demographics.

On any given Sunday morning at Holy Spirit, our three services require over one hundred volunteer ministers helping to make worship happen. In a smaller setting, only ten to twelve people may be required. Someone should organize this ministry in every church and be a true advocate for the members—not only to enable their ministry within the church, but to help them and empower them to understand their ministry at home, in the office, and on the baseball field. The point being that church size is irrelevant; all members need support and affirmation. Being a volunteer minister is more than just receiving a schedule to usher on Sundays.

Here is an overview of my job description and a few other key areas of involvement.

Coordination of Holy Spirit's Volunteer System. I work with twelve to fourteen members who each coordinate an area of worship: acolytes, communion assistants, greeters, readers, and the like. Job descriptions exist for all our volunteer positions. Generally volunteers make a two-year commitment for any position. Training for volunteers is held by the pastor, director of member ministries, or other volunteers as needed. Members sign up each year on time and talent inventories for congregational ministry. Time and talent inventories are taken each spring. The inventory also includes a large section of opportunities within the community for social service and outreach.

One of my ongoing goals is to be aware of community needs and to attempt to raise the consciousness of our members in these areas. We have recently trained several people for the Aids Outreach program, which came about by my receiving a newsletter from this organization and putting this category on the time and talent sheet. Belonging to the Society of Volunteer Administrators in our community has enabled me personally to network with directors from nonprofit, social, health-related, and other groups and to hear of their needs. It is not unusual for churches to be regularly canvassed with social service requests. We hang posters and submit articles to the weekly bulletin and newsletter, but I try to take it a step further and actually to match needs with the de-sires and talents of our ministers. Part of the joy of my position is af-firming our people for their good work, evaluating ministry, and also maintaining records of volunteer activity.

New Member Orientation. I attempt to meet with each new member throughout the course of the year. (We have three to four six-week

orientation sessions.). I schedule an individual appointment with each
person, preferably at his or her place of business. This enables me to
affirm their world ministry and to get an insight into who they are and
what gifts they might share. (Not infrequently new members' activities
in the community, in their jobs, and at home preclude commitment to
church work. I affirm and support them for their world ministries.)

   Center for Faith and Life. I act as staff liaison and resource person
in developing events and identifying event leadership. This is done by
regular attendance at the board meetings and offering to serve on sub-
committees to brainstorm different areas of education and programming.
Once we have established our topics (feminism, hate and violence, science and religion, and so forth), we create a month-long program incor-
porating agenda and speakers. I attempt to be a resource to this group,
offering ideas and suggestions of people to speak and facilitate.

Growing into the Job

What has proved very helpful to me in my growth as director of member
ministries is attending two national conferences on Ministry in Daily Life.
The first was held in Maryland, sponsored by the Evangelical Lutheran
Church in America. Clergy and laypeople were brought together to
brainstorm ways a church could be based on the principle of Ministry in
Daily Life. The second was the fifth annual Consultation of the Coalition for Ministry in Daily Life, held in Hartford. Both conferences re-
inforced my learning and encouraged new thinking in creative ways.
Discovering many others embracing the same philosophy was uplifting.
Hartford was particularly interesting from the standpoint that the group
represented many denominations: Catholic, Presbyterian, United Church
of Christ, Lutheran, Episcopal, American Baptist, Moravian, and so on.
We all came together on common ground: our ministry to others in the
world.

   In all of this, the learning has been immense, and because growth is
a prerequisite to my occupational life, I must say simply I love my "job"
and feel very honored and blessed to be able to do what I do. At times
there are challenges. I must remain on my toes constantly to advocate
for Ministry in Daily Life, to help members to understand this concept,
and to diplomatically maintain position when challenged on why things

are done a certain way. It is not always easy to recognize amazing talents and gifts in members, to know that they would be an incredible asset in leading our church, but then to go on to affirm them in their world work and let them go. As Christians and ministers, we must know that everything we do in Jesus' name is ministry, whether it be ironing, preparing a computer report, coaching Little League, or being part of the Endowment Action Group. It is all service to the Lord and pleasing to him.

Based on my experience thus far, what are the prerequisites for a "director of member ministries"? As I have told my story, one could say that knowledge of Ministry in Daily Life, although vastly helpful, is not critical; it can be learned. Certain things are essential, however. Recruiting skills are important, and the ability not to take the "nos" personally is essential. Interpersonal skills are key to being able to understand people, recognize gifts, affirm their ministries in the world, but also to have the ability to release and let go when the congregational ministry situation is not right for a particular member. A resilient attitude helps, as do good communication skills. Having some management skill empowers the director to be assertive when necessary. But this approach must be backed with good Christian values. It is important that the director of member ministries see his or her position as one of facilitator rather than doer. There is a great temptation to become involved in the actual ministry of the people rather than be a support or resource person. This becomes unfair to those being enabled and actually makes the director less effective.

My reason to be and central focus in all my work at Holy Spirit Church is to help its members to understand their faith connection and what God is doing in their lives the other six days—whether they be at home, work, church, or out on the tennis courts. To help them to understand how they minister and how God creates through them is total fulfillment for the director of member ministries. It is and must be the nucleus of my ministry. I see it this way. I have learned it this way. It is only when we come to know what God is doing in and through us that we will truly understand what the potential of our personal ministry is.

Another Approach

If a congregation is not large enough to support a full-time director of member ministries, the job could be divided: one volunteer to recruit members for congregational tasks and one to advocate for Ministry in Daily Life. Some congregations appoint a small committee for the Ministry in Daily Life advocacy. The important thing is that there be one person or a small group that interacts with both staff and the committees of the congregation to ensure that Ministry in Daily Life is continually integrated into all the work of the church. Otherwise, the natural tendency will be to focus entirely inward on traditional congregational concerns.

CHAPTER 8

The Challenges Ahead

> *For if those who are nothing think they are something, they deceive
> themselves.* (Galatians 6:3)

This book about Ministry in Daily Life at Holy Spirit Church is only a
status report. We would be kidding the reader and ourselves if we pre-
tended we have it all together. We are on the way, but there are many
challenges to face. This chapter will present the challenges we now see.
Only time will tell what others we must face.

An Inch Deep?

There is no doubt in our minds that the vast majority of members of the
Lutheran Church of the Holy Spirit understand the concept of Ministry in
Daily Life. They know that the Bible is very clear that all followers of
Jesus are called into a ministry that encompasses the totality of their lives.
They know that ministry is not something that only clergy do. They
know that a basic mission of our congregation is to affirm, equip, and
support our members for Ministry in Daily Life. They know all that.

The people of Holy Spirit have enthusiastically supported the varied
Ministry in Daily Life programs we offer. While the Sunday morning
Center for Faith and Life educational programs draw only about one
hundred people on any given Sunday, well over three hundred people
participate over the period of a year. Our attendance sheets show that.
The Monday Connection's breakfasts have been solidly supported for

almost ten years. The one-day Saturday seminars have always drawn a
good number of participants, as have our Wednesday night Lenten events.

But has all of this made any difference in the daily lives of our people? To what extent are members' words and actions in their homes,
their communities, and especially in their occupations now shaped by
their understanding of Ministry in Daily Life? Or do the vast majority of
them still live in that dualistic state in which what goes on in their lives
on Sunday does not connect with what goes on in their lives the rest of
the week? In short, is Ministry in Daily Life at Holy Spirit a mile wide
and an inch deep? I have asked that question a number of times. It is an
uncomfortable question for those of us who are in leadership positions,
but it is a very important question. It immediately leads to another question: How can we determine the depth of daily life ministry among our
members?

In the old paradigm when clergy did the ministry of the congregation and the members were passive pew sitters who paid to have that
ministry done, we had commonly accepted measurements for the effec-
tiveness of clergy ministry: numbers. To what extent was the congregation growing in membership? To what extent was financial support increasing each year? Those were the big ones. Then there were secondary measurements: How many calls does the pastor make to the sick and
shut-ins? to potential members? to marginal members? What percent of
the membership worships regularly? How many sermons were preached
and classes taught? The quality of sermons and teaching was secondary
to the pastor's performance in the primary measures of ministry. We
were once in a congregation with a pastor who had very poor sermons
and teaching skills, but he was great at raising money and that was his
salvation.

Some of our people point to our membership growth as proof that
Ministry in Daily Life is important to people. The U.S. Census data for
our major postal zone indicates that from 1980 to 1990, the general
population increased 11.2 percent. In that same period of time, our net
con-gregational membership grew 51.9 percent, seemingly five times
faster than the general population. However, because our membership
comes from other postal zones, an exact comparison cannot be made.
In any event, we have a fairly fast-growing congregation compared to
other churches nearby. Can it be attributed to Ministry in Daily Life,
our active youth program, our one contemporary worship service, or a

very friendly congregation? Probably they all contribute. But membership growth does not get at the question of how Ministry in Daily Life is playing out in the everyday activities of our people.

Determining how effective our Ministry in Daily Life programs are in shaping the words and deeds of our people during the week is one of several challenges that face us at Holy Spirit. Why should we concern ourselves with trying to deal with this issue? Is it anybody's business how I carry out my ministry in daily life? Nobody ever cared to ask me about such a private matter before.

Ah, yes, but things are changing. Under the old model of the church, the laity were passive pew sitters who were sometimes admonished to take their Christian faith into the world, but no attention was being given to how that can really happen. For the first thirty years of my life, I was never asked by a pastor, a church school teacher, a committee chair person, or a fellow member of my congregation how my ministry in daily life was going. Never.

But if a congregation is working at affirming, equipping, and supporting its people for Christian ministry in and to the world, we need to get feedback. Are we providing the necessary help? What ministry is going well? What is not? As this book is being written, we are in the process of developing a "think tank" group that will try to help us determine if Ministry in Daily Life at Holy Spirit is more than an inch deep. Will the usual survey forms and focus group discussions do the job, or is there some other way?

Bible Literacy

Another area in which we know some of our people are an inch deep is in knowledge of the Bible. But the situation is mixed. Some of our people have a very good knowledge of the Bible; some are virtually Bible illiterates. To some extent, it tends to divide along age lines. At Holy Spirit, those over fifty are generally much better versed in the Bible than those under fifty. This is typical of many congregations.

Reference was made earlier in this book to a survey conducted among the Sunday morning regulars at our Center for Faith and Life. Among these, the most faithful members in our adult education programs, 64 percent seldom or never read the Bible, while 14 percent were daily readers, and 22 percent read it at least once a week. The over-60 age group was the highest in the daily reading.

This brings up an interesting question: Is it necessary to have a good knowledge of the Bible in order to carry out Ministry in Daily Life? On the one hand, how can we ask the question, What would Jesus have me do in this situation? if we have little or no knowledge of Jesus. On the other hand, one can argue that the early Apostolic church grew by leaps and bounds without the benefit of a written New Testament and with only the conviction of who Jesus was and some knowledge of what Jesus said. In my experience, people who have only passing familiarity with the Bible question whether it is necessary to know any more of the Old Testament than the Genesis story and the Ten Commandments. They might also wonder, in order to carry out one's Ministry in Daily Life, does a person need to know anything about the Book of Acts or the Epistles? All of which causes me to ask, specifically what knowledge of the Bible is needed for a person to carry out his/her ministry in daily life? I have put this question to some of our small groups, our church staff, and a theological work group with which I maintain an ongoing relationship. Their responses will have to wait for another book.

It is interesting to observe that when we offer a study on a *book* of the Bible, we usually get a poor turnout. The majority of people are over fifty. However, when we offer a session or two of Bible study in connection with a program being presented in our Center for Faith and Life, there is a very large turnout. We recently completed an eight-week program on hate and violence in America. For the first two sessions, we imported a teaching theologian from a nearby college to lead off with a study of what the Bible has to say about hate and violence. The room was packed with about ninety people. When we ran a six-week study of a draft of our national church's proposed statement, "The Church and Human Sexuality," we imported another teaching theologian to begin by giving us two weeks of what the Bible has to say about sexuality, marriage, homosexuality, and abusive sex. Again, the room was packed with over one hundred people. Similarly, we had teaching the-ologians for our series on feminism and on handling grief. All of which suggests that Bible study related to current issues is of interest, while the traditional study of books of the Bible is not.

As much as possible, we try to introduce Bible study into the topics we present, but sometimes the Bible study is very thin. For example, when we get into public policy issues such as health care, our school system, or the welfare system, only sundry Bible verses can be introduced. The same thing applies for studies on "technomania," work addiction, and medical ethics.

Is this the way to teach the Bible today—by citing its relevance to topics being presented? Or should we continue to press for the traditional study of books of the Bible? It is a topic we debate on the board of our Center for Faith and Life as we try to deal with an area where we know some of our people are an inch deep—knowledge of the Bible.

Identity

A third challenge that faces us is to help our people truly understand that our identity is not shaped by the world; it is based on our relationship with God.

As mentioned earlier in this book, about 55 percent of our congregation is in the 30-to-55 age bracket, as compared to 36.5 percent of the American population in 1990. This is the age bracket in which career advancement is greatest and earning power follows along. We also have many technical and professional people, and two wage earners per family is the norm.

In an age when job security is no longer assured due to corporate mergers, downsizing, and productivity campaigns, young people casually say they expect to work for six or seven different employers in their working years. They do not expect job security, they say. But as families move through the 30-to-55 period, job security does become more important. With large mortgages on big homes and children going to college, the loss of even one wage earner's job can be catastrophic. Equally troublesome is the transfer of one of the partners to a distant city. Can the other partner find work there? And with single parent families, job security is a survival issue. There is a good deal of apprehension among our so-called boomers. In fact, fear permeates the entire work force today. Those who survive a downsizing live in fear of being victims in the next one. And they generally have a heavier workload because many employers cut the work force but not the work.

The result of all this is that many people feel stressed out, frightened, and insecure. The job becomes the focus of one's life. When the economic survival of the family is dependent upon the job, one's identity is wrapped up in that job. Without a job, one has no identity. Losing a job can be devastating.

Similarly, those workers over fifty-five can also become victims of job loss through "sweeteners" that encourage early retirement. The common advice is to accept an early retirement incentive or else run the risk of becoming a victim of a work force reduction. But here again, a worker who is probably at his or her earning peak with significant job responsibilities suddenly becomes "a nothing," a "worthless" person in his or her own eyes.

It is not extreme to say that today one's identity and one's sense of worth is tied up in what one does. Without work, there is no identity. All this is perfectly understandable, but it flies in the face of what we proclaim in church on Sunday. The Christian faith proclaims that all the baptized are of great worth to God. God loves us and accepts us without any merit of our own. We do not work our way into God's love. It is freely given. Amazing grace!

The principle of justification by faith was one of the great gifts of the Reformation. As a young monk, Martin Luther worked constantly to make himself good enough for God, but to no avail. He was tormented by the knowledge that he could never do enough. It was not until he fully understood the meaning of Romans 3:24 ("But by the free gift of God's grace, all are put right with him through Christ Jesus," TEV) that he realized the wonderful gift he was given.

It is difficult enough to believe fully in the amazing grace of God when one's daily work is running along smoothly. Even then our identity is defined by what we do and our worth is determined by how well we do it. But when our work, our identity, perhaps even our family's survival is threatened, it is especially difficult to say, "Yes, but, in God's eyes I am a person of great worth." It is even more difficult to speak convincingly to a desperate coworker of the grace of God. Yet that is precisely the Gospel message that ministers in daily life need to proclaim on the other side of the boundary between church and world.

The identity problem is not peculiar to the people of Holy Spirit Church by any means. It infects the whole Christian church because the grace of God seems just too good to be true. We recognize at Holy Spirit that we must keep pounding away at it. Our people must be able to cross the boundary into a world of works with the certainty that their worth is secure. They need to find ways to communicate this assurance with those whose identity is totally tied up in their work. This is one of the most difficult challenges we face. We have not yet begun to work on this other than through sermons and Bible study, and much more needs to be done.

Spirituality

One of the "in" words of the decade of the 1990s has been "spirituality." The word enjoys a great breadth of understanding, ranging from a monastic style of life to a way of energizing a business organization. Unfortunately, those who use the word frequently assume that everyone else knows exactly what it means. As a result, people often talk past each other as they use the word "spirituality" in their conversation.

At Holy Spirit, there is a need to deal with the issue of spirituality in its variety of forms. Parker Palmer, in his book *The Active Life: A Spirituality of Work, Creativity, and Caring,* provides a useful way of looking at spirituality.[11] He points out that the current understanding of spirituality "has been profoundly shaped by monastic metaphors and practices: silence, solitude, contemplation, centeredness." This "monastic spirituality" is the aspiration of many people who live in a harried world of action. For those who can arrange to get away or devote specific times each day for contemplation, the monastic style can be very meaningful. The problem is that the demands placed upon active people seem to make such withdrawal impossible. Consequently, they feel guilty about not being able to achieve the monastic style of spirituality that they suppose to be the norm. Palmer claims, however, that contemplation and action ought never to be at war with each other.

The spirituality of work is a theme lifted up by Pope John Paul II in his encyclical *On Human Work.* In the final sentences he wrote, "Let the Christian who listens to the living word of God, uniting work with prayer, know the place his work has not only in earthly progress but also in the development of the kingdom of God, to which we are all called through the power of the Holy Spirit and through the word of the Gospel."[12]

William Droel and Gregory F. Augustine Pierce have been active leaders among the Roman Catholic laity in speaking about the spirituality of work. In their book *Confident and Competent: A Challenge for the Lay Church*, they write, "Daily work can unite the sacred and secular in genuine Christian spirituality." And again, "Rather than implying overtly religious acts, spirituality should refer to the integration of faith into the concrete circumstances of a person's life."[13] While Droel and Augustine Pierce appear to reject the monastic style of spirituality, Parker Palmer argues that a contemplative and an active spirituality are not mutually exclusive.

We need to make this point with our people at Holy Spirit Church who long for a greater sense of God's presence in their lives. There are alternative approaches to spirituality: the monastic style and the active life. Both are equally valid. I know from my own experience that it is not easy to see God's presence amid the fast-paced events of a busy day. It is much easier in the seclusion of our summer home on the lake. But we need to become more assured that there is a spiritual dimension to our daily work.

As this book is being written, Pastor Al is on a three-month sabbatical leave devoted to the issue of spirituality. We anticipate that with his return we will be better able to help our people who long for a greater sense of God's presence in their daily lives.

Telling Our Story

As indicated earlier in this book, many of us are uncomfortable talking to others about our faith. In the survey of our Center for Faith and Life regulars, only 34 percent said, "I feel comfortable talking about my faith with strangers." If we are to carry our faith into daily life, we need to be able to talk about it in a manner that is comfortable for us and welcoming to a stranger. The new format of our parish newsletter, featuring front-page stories about faith journeys written by *our own* people, should begin to free us to talk with others.

Real-Life Experiences

A part of the mission statement of our Center for Faith and Life is that we "deepen Christian faith through education, support, and real-life experiences . . ." Most of our learning through "real-life experiences" is confined to the type of people we are—suburban, upper-middle-class, business, and professional people. We have very little exposure to people who live on the margins of society—the poor, the immigrant, the homeless, the social outcasts. Our members get minimal exposure to people who are different from them through our partnership with the congregation of St. Martin de Porres, the only Lutheran Hispanic congregation in the Lehigh Valley. We must always be careful that we do not overwhelm the tiny congregation with support and thereby become paternalistic. Some of our people serve as volunteers in social service agencies like the food kitchens, Meals on Wheels, the Sixth Street Shelter, and others. Considering the size of our congregation, however, we need to expose more people to the reality of how less fortunate people live. Given the busy lives most of our members have, it is a challenge to provide this exposure.

Lifestyle

Jesus had a very simple lifestyle as far as possessions go. He once said, "Foxes have holes, and birds of the air have nests, but the Son of Man has nowhere to lay his head" (Matt. 8:20). He warned against worrying about food and clothing because, he said, "Where your treasure is, there your heart will be also" (Luke 12:34). At his death, soldiers cast lots for his only clothing and he was placed in a borrowed tomb. The early church, likewise, had little concern for personal possessions. In Acts we read, "Now the whole group of those who believed were of one heart and soul, and no one claimed private ownership of any possessions, but everything they owned was held in common" (Acts 4:32). Throughout the ages, a simple lifestyle has been a hallmark of many faithful Christians.

And how is it with us today? Is there any discernible difference between Christians and non-Christians when it comes to possessions? Princeton sociologist Robert Wuthnow says there isn't. In his book *God and Mammon in America*, he claims that Christians in America are spiritually adrift when it comes to the realm of personal economics. In an article on the subject, he concludes "that the evidence suggests that faith makes little difference to the ways in which people actually conduct their financial affairs."[14]

Wuthnow's statement is certainly true for the vast majority of us at Holy Spirit. The mix of cars on our parking lot is no different than that at any large shopping mall. We dress the same as the rest of society and eat at the same or perhaps better restaurants. We live in large homes, some with swimming pools. Some of us belong to exclusive clubs.

We need to ask whether our lifestyle gets in the way of our ministry in daily life. This is an awkward question to ponder because we fear we know what the answer might be. Nevertheless, we need to examine our lifestyles if we claim to be the follower of one whose style was very simple. We have touched upon this subject in our Center for Faith and Life, but it is not a popular one with our people. Yet we cannot ignore dealing with lifestyle.

Miles to Go

While much of this book gives details of how far we have come with Ministry in Daily Life, this chapter says convincingly that we are only on the way. We confess that we are not certain of the degree to which our people are actually carrying out their ministries in daily life. We confess that many of our people have a poor knowledge of the Bible, but at the same time, we confess we are not certain of the degree to which biblical literacy is needed for Ministry in Daily Life. We confess that we face a monumental task of helping our people attain such a firm sense of iden-tity, through the Grace of God, that they can minister to those on the other side of the boundaries. We confess that we need to help people more with their spirituality and with freely talking about their faith with strangers. We confess that we need to have more contact with people who live on the margin. And, finally, we confess that we have not yet worked out the issue of Christian lifestyle for Ministry in Daily Life. This book has been a status report on how Ministry in Daily Life has become an integral part of the mission and ministry of our congregation, but there is much more ahead of us.

In his wonderful book *God's Frozen People*, Mark Gibbs offers these words:

> Certainly there will be great risks in a Christianity of genuine worldliness, for it means living in the open air, it means living with [people] and serving them in all those areas where Christ is never named, though they belong to him, or where he is named only to be understood or reviled.[15]

As the people of Holy Spirit Church daily cross the boundaries into a world that is largely indifferent and sometimes hostile, we go with the assurance that Ministry in Daily Life is no longer just a program of our church. It *is* the church.

CHAPTER 9

We Are Called

This book has been written with the conviction that, for a variety of soci-
ological reasons, the mission and ministry of the Christian church in the
twenty-first century will fall on the shoulders of the laity. The good
news is that the Christian laity are already located in strategic positions
to carry out this ministry—in offices, factories, homes, schools, government—in short, in the world. The bad news is that the Christian laity
have been raised in a church in which they have been largely passive. It
is a church that has urged the laity to become active exclusively in congregational life and has left them to fend for themselves in their weekday
world.

The precipitous drop in membership in mainline denominations over
the past thirty years makes it clear that unless congregations make a radical change in how ministry is done, they themselves are at risk. But even
if the denominations were still doing well, Ministry in Daily Life would
be necessary for an authentic Christianity. Jesus asked his disciples to
follow him. We do not follow Jesus if we maintain a dualism between
our Sunday experiences and the experiences of the rest of the week.
Jesus has sent us into the world.

It appears at this moment that the change in the organization or
structure of the Christian church in America will not need to be radical.
We will still have congregations and ordained clergy. The only difference is that the focus will be on affirming, equipping, and supporting
individual members for their ministries in the world. We will still have
seminaries. The only difference is that they will train future clergy to do
ministry *through* the members of the congregation. We will still have
some sort of denominational structures. The only difference is that they
will focus their efforts on the things that individual congregations cannot

do. At least that's the way we see it at the Lutheran Church of the Holy Spirit.

The radical change will be in the way we do ministry. The overwhelming number of laity and clergy in American churches do not truly understand Ministry in Daily Life. If you were to ask the members of a typical congregation how they are affirmed, equipped, and supported by their church for the ministries in daily life, the first response would be that they don't think the church is supposed to help them in their daily work. That was the finding of a very large survey conducted by the National Council of Churches a few years ago.

We know from experience that it will not be easy for laity to embrace Ministry in Daily Life. It has been very comfortable to worship God on Sunday and not to carry the Christian faith into the weekday world. When the laity have heard the words "Go into all the world and proclaim the good news to the whole creation" (Mark 16:15), it has meant that someone else, a foreign missionary, has that job, and all the laity have to do is give money.

Now, however, when the "world" is right outside the doors of the church building and the laity are called to do ministry in and to the world, things aren't as comfortable—or as clear. What does Jesus mean when he prays for his followers to be in but not of the world (John 17:13-18)? Jesus says we should turn the other cheek (Luke 6:29). (Seriously? Even for muggers?) He says, "Give to everyone who begs from you" (John 6:30). (Give money to winos on the street? Lend to my enemy and expect nothing back?) Incredible! Doing Jesus' bidding—ministry —is certainly going to be difficult for the laity.

Embracing Ministry in Daily Life will be difficult for some clergy, too. They will feel reluctant to share the function of ministry with the congregation. Some will think their authority will be undermined if everyone is a minister. Those who were taught to use a controlling style of leadership will wonder, How can I possibly control all these people if everyone is running around doing ministry? For pastors who have worked hard to get people involved in the work of the *church*, getting people involved in ministry in the *world* will require a dramatic shift in thinking.

It would be much easier for both laity and clergy to continue traditional ways of doing ministry. But we have been called. The Holy Spirit is calling Christians to active mission and ministry in the world, to a new

style of ministry for the society in which we live. As we enter the
twenty-first century, we cannot ignore the call.

NOTES

1. Loren Mead, *The Once and Future Church: Reinventing the Congregation for a New Mission Frontier* (Bethesda, Md.: The Alban Institute, 1991), 68.

2. William Easum, *Sacred Cows Make Gourmet Burgers: Ministry Anytime, Anywhere by Anyone* (Nashville: Abingdon Press, 1995).

3. Davida Foy Crabtree, *The Empowering Church: How One Congregation Supports Lay People's Ministries in the World* (Bethesda, Md.: The Alban Institute, 1989).

4. Tex Sample, *U.S. Lifestyles and Mainline Churches* (Louisville, Ky.: Westminster John Knox Press, 1990), 114.

5. Mead, *The Once and Future Church*, 76.

6. *Constitutions, Bylaws, and Continuing Resolutions: Evangelical Lutheran Church in America* (Chicago: Evangelical Lutheran Church in America, 1991), 7.11.

7. Elton Trueblood, *The Incendiary Fellowship* (New York: Harper and Row, 1967), 52.

8. Gerhard Ebeling, *Luther: An Introduction to His Thought* (Philadelphia: Fortress Press, 1964), 212.

9. Suzanne Farnham, *Listening Hearts: Discerning Call in Community* (Ridgefield, Conn.: Morehouse, 1991).

10. Trueblood, *Fellowship*, 41.

11. Parker Palmer, *The Active Life: A Spirituality of Work, Creativity, and Caring* (SanFrancisco: HarperSanFrancisco, 1990), 1.

12. William Droel and Gregory F. Augustine Pierce, *Confident and Competent: A Challenge for the Lay Church* (Notre Dame, Ind.: Ave Maria Press, 1987), 41n.

13. Ibid., 43.

14. Robert Wuthnow, "Pious Materialism: How Americans View Faith and Money," *Christianity Today*, March 3, 1993.

15. Mark Gibbs, *God's Frozen People* (Philadelphia: Westminster, 1965), 186.

Resources

Had this appendix been attempted forty years ago, in the church heydays of the 1950s, it would have offered a *very* short listing of resources. A few of the Elton Trueblood books were on sale, and the landmark book by Hendrik Kraemer, *A Theology of the Laity*, appeared in 1958. None of the resource lists, group study programs, newsletters, magazines, or books listed in this chapter—nor anything like them—were in existence. This is one more indication that the Holy Spirit is breathing new life into the Christian church and that new life is the ministry of the laity.

Three caveats are necessary for this appendix. First, many resources such as study programs and books have a limited shelf life, as determined by the publisher. Listed in this chapter are resources available in 1996 and their prices. Second, the names of contact persons may change also, but the organizations with which they are affiliated probably will not. Third, not all the resources listed have been tested by the author; therefore, the quality of a few of them is uncertain.

Where to Seek Help

The Alban Institute, 4550 Montgomery Avenue, Suite 433N, Bethesda, MD 20814-3341. 800/486-1318.

The institute specializes in supporting congregations. Over the years they have produced many books and articles and have conducted numerous conferences and seminars. A call to Alban may produce the resources you are seeking.

The Coalition for Ministry in Daily Life, 4694 Boxwood Circle, Emmaus, PA 18049. 610/965-3259.

This fledgling international, ecumenical organization is a partnership of Ministry in Daily Life resource persons from the major denominations, seminaries, local judicatories, congregations/parishes, publishers, and independent centers. Its goals are to share resources, work cooperatively, plan events, assist congregations, and develop an information and referral service that will directly provide people with resources or tell them where to go. Call to become a partner or for more information.

The Lutheran Church of the Holy Spirit, 3461 South Cedar Crest Boulevard, Emmaus, PA 18049. 610/967-2220.

For further information on any of the Holy Spirit programs or concepts, contact Ms. Pam Bonina, Director of Member Ministries. Pam and our pastors are happy to share information. We see that as part of our mission as a congregation.

Denominational Offices

Depending upon your needs, your denomination's national office may either have the resource you seek or refer you to another source. The following denominations are known to have specific Ministry in Daily Life staff assignments.

American Baptist Churches, National Ministries, P.O. Box 851, Valley Forge, PA 19482-0851. 215/768-2412. *Contact:* David Laubach.

The Episcopal Church, Congregational Ministries Cluster, 815 Second Avenue, New York, NY 10017-4594. 212/867-8400.

The Evangelical Lutheran Church in America, Division for Ministry, 8765 West Higgins Road, Chicago, IL 60631. 312/380-2874. *Contact:* Sally Simmel.

The Presbyterian Church (U.S.A.), National Ministries Division, 100 Witherspoon Street, Louisville, KY 40202-1396. 502/569-5753. *Contact:* Judith Atwell.

The United Church of Christ, Board of Homeland Ministries, 700 Prospect Avenue, Cleveland, OH 44115-1100. 216/736-3797.

United Methodist Church, Congregations and Community Action Ministries, P.O. Box 840, Nashville, TN 37202. 615/340-7144. *Contact:* Alyne JoAnn Eslinger.

Lists of Resources

Marketplace Ministries, InterVarsity Christian Fellowship, has put together an annotated list of over two-hundred "best books" as resources for ministry related to work. Some books are Christian in nature; others are among the best secular books on various aspects of work. For the latest list, contact: Pete Hammond or Jay Baldwin, Marketplace Ministries, InterVarsity Christian Fellowship, 6400 Schroeder Road, P.O. Box 7895, Madison, WI 53707-7895. 608/274-9001. Price: $25.00.

"This Call's For You" is an attractive brochure prepared by the Presbyterian Church (U.S.A.). It focuses on vocation that "gives meaning to our daily routine." It lists adult programs, as well as programs for children in various age groups and junior and senior high youth. There's not much out there for children and youth. For a copy of the brochure, write: Judith D. Atwell, National Ministries Division, Presbyterian Church (U.S.A.), 100 Witherspoon Street, Louisville, KY 40202-1396. 502/569-5753.

The Whole Ministry Catalog: Resources for Transforming Ministry is a forty-page annotated list of group study resources, books, newsletters, audiovisuals, and other types of resources. Many of the items, but by no means all, originated with the Evangelical Lutheran Church in America. However, this catalog is the best overall list of resources that we know of. It is updated every few years. Division for Congregational Ministries, Evangelical Lutheran Church in America, 8765 West Higgins Road, Chicago, IL 60631. Price: $3.00, includes postage and handling.

Working: Making a Difference in God's World, by Carol Weiser, Sally Simmel, and Bob Sitze, is a wonderful source book for affirming, equipping, and supporting Christians in their ministries in the workplace. The

final section of this loose-leaf book contains a list of various types of
resources, but other sections of the book deal with models, programs,
stories, and ideas. The notebook also contains suggestions for devotions,
prayers, and even a sermon. Augsburg Fortress, Publishers, 426 South
Fifth Street, Box 1209, Minneapolis, MN 55440-1209. 800/328-4648.
Price (including an audiocassette): $25.75, plus postage and handling.
Bulletin inserts on the same theme tell stories of twelve "ordinary Christians ministries." Price: $8.80 per set of 25 copies of each of the 12
inserts, plus postage and handling.

Group Study Programs

Connections: Faith And World by Norma J. Everist and Nelvin Vos
    A thirty-session adult study course based on Luther's Large Cat-
echism. Through a variety of learning experiences, including visiting
participants' workplaces, members learn how their faith and daily life
connect. As this book is going to press, the course is being significantly
revised. Materials in the original course, however, include a 112-page
participant notebook, a 176-page leader guide, and an interactive video.
Contact: Director for Ministry in Daily Life, Evangelical Lutheran
Church in America, 8765 West Higgins Road, Chicago, IL 60631. 312/
380-2874. An updated version will be available in 1996. Price: Unknown.

Ministry in Daily Life: A Guide to Living the Baptismal Covenant by
Linda L. Grenz and J. Fletcher Lowe Jr.
    Contains articles, suggestions, and resources to help congregations
support the ministries their members do at work, school, home, in communities, leisure time, retirement, and every aspect of day-to-day life.
Episcopal Parish Services, P.O. Box 269, William Penn Annex, Philadelphia, PA 19105-0269. 800/903-5544.

Our Reasonable Service by Harry C. Griffith
    A program designed to involve the whole congregation in ministry.
It starts with the basics and moves into ongoing education for ministry
both in the church and in the world. Published by Adventures in Ministry, P.O. Box 81746, Bakersfield, CA 93380. 805/588-8869. Prices:
Leader's Guide, $50.00; "Discovering My Ministry" workbook, $5.00.

A Place For Faith by Diana Sickles
   A thirteen-session study course that helps adults explore the wide variety of daily situations that present opportunities for ministry to others. Augsburg Fortress Publishers, 426 South Fifth Street, Box 1209, Minneapolis, MN 55440-1209. 800/328-4648. Price: Participant's Book, $3.95; Leader's Guide, $4.95.

Renewing God's People by Susan Gillies and Ingrid Dvemak
   Contains a variety of group studies and action plans for worship, education, and outreach. Also contains prayer meditation suggestions and a small annotated bibliography. National Ministries, American Baptist Churches, P.O. Box 851, Valley Forge, PA 19482-0851. Or call: David Laubach, 215/768-2412. Price: $5.95.

Vocation: Basic Resource Packet
   A variety of resources, including group study programs, are available from the United Church of Christ. There are too many items to list here, but a list of resources can be obtained by writing: The United Church of Christ, Board of Homeland Ministries, 700 Prospect Avenue, Cleveland, OH 44115-1100. Or call: Verlyn L. Barker, 216/736-3797.

Newsletters

The Call
   A Ministry in Daily Life quarterly newsletter primarily directed at members of the Evangelical Lutheran Church in America but containing good essays on Ministry in Daily Life. Director for Ministry in Daily Life, Evangelical Lutheran Church in America, 8765 West Higgins Road, Chicago 60631. 312/380-2874.

Connections
   A monthly letter from Barbara Wendland with her musings on the role of the laity in the church and in the world. She is coauthor with Stanley Menking of the book *God's Partners: Lay Christians at Work* (see "Books," below). 505 Cherokee Drive, Temple, TX 76504.

Initiatives
   A semi-monthly newsletter of the National Center for the Laity,

which is "in support of the Christian in the World." Contains articles about Christians in the workplace, reports on new books, and announcements of forthcoming events. This is one of the major contributions of the Roman Catholic laity. 205 West Monroe Street, #300, Chicago, IL 60606.

Inside Marketplace

A bimonthly newsletter published by InterVarsity Christian Fellowship. Contains essays, announcements, book reviews, and news items relating to ministry in the marketplace. InterVarsity Christian Fellowship, 6400 Schroeder Road, P.O. Box 7895, Madison, WI 53707-7895. 608/274-9001.

Laynet

A newsletter of the Coalition for Ministry in Daily Life (see "Where to Seek Help," above). Contains lists of resources, announcements of forthcoming events, "think pieces," and personal helps. Published three times a year.

Links

A monthly newsletter containing essays, announcements, and book reports. General Board of Discipleship, United Methodist Church, Laity in Ministry, P.O. Box 840, Nashville, TN 37202-0840.

Ministry of the Laity in the Workplace

A quarterly newsletter that focuses primarily on carrying out ministry in one's place of work. American Baptist Churches, National Ministries, P.O. Box 851, Valley Forge, PA 19482-0851.

Ministry of Money

This provocative newsletter focuses on how we use our money, which is an important aspect of Ministry in Daily Life. Contains thoughtful articles and lists future workshops. 2 Professional Drive, Suite 220, Gaithersburg, MD 20879

Quarterly Yoke Letter

A two-page "think piece" on some aspect of faith in daily life. The Yokefellows, 228 College Avenue, Richmond, IN 47374.

Magazines

Faith at Work

   A long-standing, quarterly magazine of "resources for growing Christians." Contains essays, editorial reflections, announcements of F.A.W. conferences, Bible studies, poems, prayers. 150 South Washington Street, #204, Falls Church, VA 22046-2921.

The Marketplace

   A bimonthly magazine "for Christians in business." Generally has a theme each issue. Articles, study suggestions, "think pieces," and book reports. The Mennonite Economic Development Associates (MEDA), 616 Walnut Avenue, Scottdale, PA 15683.

Books

One of the old maxims of management training people is, "All development is self-development." There is an element of truth in this statement for those who are claiming their ministries in daily life. All the affirming, equipping, and supporting that a congregation can offer will not be enough unless people themselves assume some responsibility for their own ministry development. Books on specific aspects of Ministry in Daily Life are essential to a person's self-development, especially for those who belong to a congregation that pays little or no attention to the total ministry of the total church.

   Books opened the doors to me in the years when "lay ministry" meant little more than assisting the pastor in his ministry. (In most denominations, there were no female clergy then.) The books of Elton Trueblood, a wonderful Quaker author, gradually led me to see the broad expanses of Christian ministry. But it was Mark Gibbs, an Anglican advocate for the laity, who blew the gates wide open with his book *God's Frozen People* and its sequel, *God's Lively People*. Without the books of those two departed authors, I would not be writing this book today. Unfortunately, most of their books are no longer in print.

   The growth of the lay movement can certainly be measured by the number of books that are available on the topic. From only a handful following the end of World War II, the number has increased to hundreds, possibly thousands. They cover all aspects of a Christian's ministry in daily life, from business ethics formulations to spiritual formation, from political life to prayer life, from pietism to materialism.

Obviously, it is impossible to offer a comprehensive list of all these books, even if I knew them all. What is offered here are current books that have impressed me. They are confined to two general categories: books on the basic concepts of ministry in daily life and those that focus more on ministry in the workplace. The first group helps the beginner get a firmer grasp on daily life ministry. The second grouping deals with the arena where the boundaries are many and the walls are high: the workplace. To the best of my knowledge, all of the books listed are still available.

Ministry Basics

Banks, Robert. *Redeeming the Routines: Bringing Theology to Life.* Wheaton, Ill.: Bridgepoint-Victor, 1993.

By truly bringing theology "down to earth," Banks helps Christians connect faith with the experiences of daily life.

Benne, Robert. *Ordinary Saints.* Minneapolis: Augsburg Fortress, 1988.

A good basic book on Ministry in Daily Life.

Crabtree, Davida Foy. *The Empowering Church: How One Congregation Supports Lay People's Ministries in the World.* Bethesda, Md.: The Alban Institute, 1989.

The subtitle describes this book well.

Diehl, William. *The Monday Connection: On Being an Authentic Christian in a Weekday World.* San Francisco: Harper SanFrancisco, 1991.

Five ways a person carries Christian ministry into daily life.

Diehl, William. *Thank God, It's Monday!* Minneapolis: Augsburg Publishing House, 1982.

How a Christian deals with the daily issues of materialism, competition, status-seeking, and power. Presented through stories and first-person accounts.

Droel, William L., and Gregory F. Augustine Pierce. *Confident and Competent: A Challenge for the Lay Church.* Notre Dame, Ind.: Ave Maria Press, 1987.

A challenge for laypeople to fulfill the mandate of the Second Vatican Council "to be the church in the world."

Farnham, Suzanne, Joseph P. Gill, R. Taylor McLean, and Susan M. Ward. *Listening Hearts: Discovering Call in Community.* Harrisburg, Pa.: Morehouse Publishing, 1991.

A process for discerning one's call in daily life within the context of a small Christian community.

Mead, Loren B. *The Once and Future Church: Reinventing the Congregation for a New Mission Frontier.* Bethesda, Md.: The Alban Institute, 1991.

This best-selling book describes the context in which ministry in daily life will have to take place in the twenty-first century.

Mead, Loren B. *Transforming Congregations for the Future.* Bethesda, Md.: The Alban Institute, 1994.

Mead gives further detail of the context in which ministry by laypersons must take place in the twenty-first century.

Palmer, Parker J. *The Active Life: Wisdom for Work, Creativity, and Caring.* SanFrancisco: HarperSanFrancisco, 1990.

A fine book on spirituality for active people.

Menking, Stanley J., and Barbara Wendland. *God's Partners: Lay Christians at Work.* Valley Forge, Pa.: Judson Press, 1993.

An interesting dialogue between an active layperson and a theologian on issues basic to the Christian life.

Stevens, R. Paul. *Disciplines of the Hungry Heart: Christians Living Seven Days a Week.* LaBelle, Fla.: Shaw Publishing, 1993.

Deals with how a person in these hectic times balances schedules and needs with the pursuit of spiritual growth.

Ministry in the Workplace

Banks, Robert. *God The Worker: Journeys into the Mind, Heart and Imagination of God.* Valley Forge, Pa.: Judson Press, 1992.
Using the Bible as a guidebook, Banks explores dynamic images of God at work.

Banks, Robert. *Faith Goes to Work: Reflections from the Marketplace.* Bethesda, Md.: The Alban Institute, 1993.
A collection of articles written by a television journalist, banker, teacher, farmer, and others describing how they relate their faith to their daily work.

Hardy, Lee. *The Fabric of this World: Inquiries into Calling, Career Choice, and the Design of Human Work.* Grand Rapids, Mich.: Wm. B. Eerdmans Publishing, 1990.
An exploration of the historic view of work and the influence exerted by the Protestant Reformers.

Kowalski, Judith, and Dean Collins. *To Serve and Protect: Law Enforcement Officers Reflect on Their Faith and Work.* Minneapolis: Augsburg Fortress; Chicago: ACTA, 1992.
One of the series, "The Christian at Work in the World." Available from ACTA Publications, 4848 North Clark Street, Chicago, IL 60640.

Pierce, Gregory F. Augustine. *Of Human Hands: A Reader in the Spirituality of Work.* Minneapolis: Augsburg Fortress; Chicago: ACTA, 1991.
Christians from a wide range of occupations and experiences share their insights into the spirituality of their own work. One of the series, "The Christian at Work in the World." Available from ACTA Publications, 4848 North Clark Street, Chicago, IL 60640.

Rion, Michael. *The Responsible Manager: Practical Strategies for Ethical Decision Making.* New York: Harper and Row, 1990.
A business ethicist and former president of Hartford Seminary writes about ethical decision making. Without using the word "Christian," Rion writes an ethics book with solid Christian values for the business community.

Sherman, Doug, and William Hendricks. *Your Work Matters to God.* Colorado Springs, Colo.: NavPress, 1990.

Presents a liberating theology of work and goes on to deal with many workplace issues facing Christians.

Slattery, Patrick. *Caretakers of Creation: Farmers Reflect on their Faith and Work.* Minneapolis: Augsburg Fortress; Chicago: ACTA, 1991.

Men and women from rural America tell their stories and share their insights on the connections between faith and farming. One of the series, "The Christian at Work in the World." Available from ACTA Publications, 4848 North Clark Street, Chicago, IL 60640.

Sorensen, David, and Barbara DeGrote Sorensen. *Kindling the Spark: A Dialog with Christian Teachers on Their Work.* Minneapolis: Augsburg Fortress; Chicago: ACTA, 1992.

Teachers speak of their ministry in the workplace. One of the series on "The Christian at Work in the World." Available from ACTA Publications, 4848 North Clark Street, Chicago, IL 60640.

Spirituality of Work Series

Each short booklet features the reflections of persons in a particular field of work. The present booklets include nurses, teachers, homemakers, lawyers, business people, and unemployed workers. Available from ACTA Publications, 4848 North Clark Street, Chicago, IL 60640. Price: $2.95 per booklet.

Tucker, Graham. *The Faith-Work Connection: A Practical Application of Christian Values in the Marketplace.* Toronto: Anglican Book Centre, 1987.

Gets into practical approaches to ministry in the marketplace, especially in management.

Please note under "Lists of Resources," above, that Pete Hammond of Marketplace Ministries has an annotated list of over two hundred "best books" relating in various ways to Ministry in Daily Life. If you would like more book suggestions, why not write to Pete?

The Alban Institute:
an invitation to membership

The Alban Institute, begun in 1974, believes that the congregation is essential to the task of equipping the people of God to minister in the church and the world. A multi-denominational membership organization, the Institute provides on-site training, educational programs, consulting, research, and publishing for hundreds of churches across the country.

The Alban Institute invites you to be a member of this partnership of laity, clergy, and executives–a partnership that brings together people who are raising important questions about congregational life and people who are trying new solutions, making new discoveries, finding a new way of getting clear about the task of ministry. The Institute exists to provide you with the kinds of information and resources you need to support your ministries.

Join us now and enjoy these benefits:

CONGREGATIONS: The Alban Journal, a highly respected journal published six times a year, to keep you up to date on current issues and trends.

Inside Information, Alban's quarterly newsletter, keeps you informed about research and other happenings around Alban. Available to members only.

Publications Discounts:

- ☐ 15% for Individual, Retired Clergy, and Seminarian Members
- ☐ 25% for Congregational Members
- ☐ 40% for Judiciary and Seminary Executive Members

Discounts on Training and Education Events

Write our Membership Department at the address below or call us at 1-800-486-1318 or 301-718-4407 for more information about how to join The Alban Institute's growing membership, particularly about Congregational Membership in which 12 designated persons receive all benefits of membership.

The Alban Institute, Inc.
Suite 433 North
4550 Montgomery Avenue
Bethesda, MD 20814-3341